How to Write the Perfect Federal Job Résumé & Résumé Cover Letter

WITH COMPANION CD-ROM

By Melanie Williamson

HOW TO WRITE THE PERFECT FEDERAL JOB RÉSUMÉ & RÉSUMÉ COVER LETTER: WITH COMPANION CD-ROM

Library of Congress Cataloging-in-Publication Data

Williamson, Melanie, 1981-
  How to write the perfect federal job résumé & résumé cover letter : with companion CD-ROM / by Melanie Williamson.
      p. cm.
  Includes bibliographical references and index.
  ISBN-13: 978-1-60138-320-4 (alk. paper)
  ISBN-10: 1-60138-320-7 (alk. paper)
  1. Résumés (Employment) 2. Civil service positions--United States. I. Title.
  HF5383.W474 2010
  650.14'2--dc22
                          2010044268

PROJECT MANAGER: Melissa Peterson • mpeterson@atlantic-pub.com
INTERIOR LAYOUT: Antoinette D'Amore • addesign@videotron.ca
COVER DESIGN: Jackie Miller • millerjackiej@gmail.com

Printed on Recycled Paper

Printed in the United States.

We recently lost our beloved pet "Bear," who was not only our best and dearest friend but also the "Vice President of Sunshine" here at Atlantic Publishing. He did not receive a salary but worked tirelessly 24 hours a day to please his parents. Bear was a rescue dog that turned around and showered myself, my wife, Sherri, his grandparents Jean, Bob, and Nancy, and every person and animal he met (maybe not rabbits) with friendship and love. He made a lot of people smile every day.

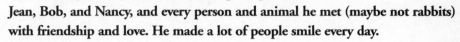

We wanted you to know that a portion of the profits of this book will be donated to The Humane Society of the United States. *–Douglas & Sherri Brown*

The human-animal bond is as old as human history. We cherish our animal companions for their unconditional affection and acceptance. We feel a thrill when we glimpse wild creatures in their natural habitat or in our own backyard.

Unfortunately, the human-animal bond has at times been weakened. Humans have exploited some animal species to the point of extinction.

The Humane Society of the United States makes a difference in the lives of animals here at home and worldwide. The HSUS is dedicated to creating a world where our relationship with animals is guided by compassion. We seek a truly humane society in which animals are respected for their intrinsic value, and where the human-animal bond is strong.

Want to help animals? We have plenty of suggestions. Adopt a pet from a local shelter, join The Humane Society and be a part of our work to help companion animals and wildlife. You will be funding our educational, legislative, investigative and outreach projects in the U.S. and across the globe.

Or perhaps you'd like to make a memorial donation in honor of a pet, friend or relative? You can through our Kindred Spirits program. And if you'd like to contribute in a more structured way, our Planned Giving Office has suggestions about estate planning, annuities, and even gifts of stock that avoid capital gains taxes.

Maybe you have land that you would like to preserve as a lasting habitat for wildlife. Our Wildlife Land Trust can help you. Perhaps the land you want to share is a backyard—that's enough. Our Urban Wildlife Sanctuary Program will show you how to create a habitat for your wild neighbors.

So you see, it's easy to help animals. And The HSUS is here to help.

2100 L Street NW • Washington, DC 20037 • 202-452-1100
www.hsus.org

DEDICATION

*I want to dedicate this book
to all my family and friends who helped me put it together.*

TABLE
OF
CONTENTS

Chapter 2: Information to Know Before Creating Your Résumé and Cover Letter 51

Chapter 4: Finding Help Through the Internet   97

Chapter 7: Designing the Perfect Cover Letter   183

INTRODUCTION

Take a moment to picture a highly trained and experienced sales person whom you have met in the past. This person might have been selling a car, furniture, time-shares, or even a house. The professional sales associate is always very confident, professional, and well dressed because sales associates understand that first impressions, as well as presentation, are very important when selling something.

Professional sales associates have well-crafted sales pitches memorized, and they are able to deliver their sales pitch with such ease and confidence that it sounds natural and unrehearsed. The sales pitch covers all of the information you need to know in order to make a purchasing decision. Sales pitches are well written and prepared well in advance of the sales associate's first interaction with the customer.

Professional sales associates have performed an extensive amount of research on both the product they are selling and the target consumer group. They know all the product information and the financing numbers to deliver immediate information and to avoid leaving the consumer with something to look up. The sales associates can answer any question the consumer might have.

Professional salespeople are also well prepared. Regardless of what reason you present for not wanting to make the purchase, the sales associate is prepared with a counter to your hesitations. The sales associate is so prepared because he or she understands that if the consumer leaves, his or her chance of making the sale dramatically decreases. The sales associate will create a situation where the consumer is convinced they cannot only afford the product, but they also cannot afford *not* to have it.

When preparing a résumé and cover letter for a federal job, it is imperative that you embrace the example of a highly trained and experienced sales associate. Your résumé and cover letter will represent you to the people in charge of making a decision that could potentially change your life. Both your résumé and cover letter should be professional, organized, and display the confidence you have in your ability to fill the position for which you are applying.

When you are describing your education, work experience, and marketable qualities, it should flow effortlessly. You are writing about your personal qualities and experiences, so you should be able to discuss those qualities and experiences as effortlessly as if you were talking to a friend. It is important to highlight the qualities that most closely relate to the position for which you are applying.

Do your research prior to preparing your résumé and cover letter. You should know everything there is to know about the position, job, description, qualifications, as well as the agency and department to which you are applying. There is an endless amount of information online covering the various federal agencies. Use that information to be as informed as possible, so that you can tailor your résumé and cover letter to the specific position.

The more prepared you are while writing your résumé and cover letter, the more apparent that will be to the people reviewing your application package. You should have all the information you need regarding past employers, years of service, and contact information. You should also have a copy of the job description available to refer back to during the writing process. Your résumé and cover letter should be perfectly organized, seamless, consistent, and tailored to the position.

CAN THIS BOOK HELP YOU?

This book is written for job seekers trying to get a job with the federal government for the first time. The content of this book will help you learn how to search for federal jobs, create the perfect résumé tailored to the specific position for which you are applying, create a cover letter that perfectly represents you as the ideal candidate for the position, and give you an understanding of the federal hiring process.

The hiring process for federal jobs is distinctively different than the hiring process in the private sector. It is longer in duration and far more intensive. The hiring process for federal jobs is also more competitive than in the private sector, with more applicants applying for each position. However, the benefits of working for the federal government are far greater than most jobs in the private sector. Those benefits will be covered in the first chapter of this book.

RECENT CHANGES IN THE FEDERAL JOB MARKET

The federal government is currently facing mass retirement by current employees due to the aging workforce. This is particularly true in law enforcement positions because the retirement age is considerably younger than other positions, even within the federal government. For example, law enforcement employees are eligible to retire at age 50 with 20 years of service. Non-law enforcement employees can only retire with 20 years of service if they are a minimum of 60 years old. A non-law enforcement employee can retire at age 55 at the youngest, but only with 30 years of service. According to a 2008 report published by the Office of Personnel Management (OPM), only approximately 24 percent of employees are still working for the federal government nine years after they become eligible for retirement. The wave of retirements is leaving a wide variety of vacancies through every department of the federal government, which need to be filled quickly to ensure the smooth running of each department.

The 2008 to 2009 economic downturn created a situation for increased hiring by the federal government. President Barack Obama's American Recovery and Reinvestment Act of 2009 created a wide variety of new jobs in the federal government and greatly expanded a number of agencies and departments. As of April 2010, slightly more than a year after the Recovery Act passed, 56 federal agencies have already been able to hire more employees. The Recovery Act has provided ample opportunities for people looking to get into a federal job. This book will help you understand the Recovery Act and the availability of jobs it has created.

The negative impact of the economy has caused an increase in work for several federal agencies, including the Department of Health and Human Services, Department of Housing and Urban Development (HUD), Department of the Treasury, and Department of Justice. There has been an increase in federal aid, as well as an increase in activity dealing with the corruption and predatory lending that contributed to the mortgage crisis.

The recent economic slump has also made federal jobs even more desirable due to the job stability they provide. The benefits for federal jobs are superior to most private sector jobs, and federal jobs are not outsourced to other counties. Although the federal job market has expanded, the perks of working for the federal government have also increased the competition for those positions.

UNDERSTANDING THE BOOK'S ORGANIZATION

The objective of this book is to not only to walk you through writing the perfect cover letter and résumé, but also to prepare you for government employment. With that objective in mind, this book will provide information covering the many agencies and types of positions available within the federal government, the wide variety of benefits available to federal employees, and the federal application process. This book will also take you beyond the résumé-writing process, explain the variety of non-tradition paths to federal employment, and what you need to know once you are hired into a federal position.

The final section of this book is the appendices. Here you will find sample résumés and cover letters, a list of agencies and departments, government pay scales, and a glossary of key terms. The appendices will be a go-to section for all the resources you will need during the federal hiring process. This book also includes a CD-ROM filled with valuable information and resources to help you once you are ready to start writing your résumé and cover letter. You will be able to use the CD-ROM to find agency websites and information. You can also turn to the CD-ROM for additional examples of résumés and cover letters used by federal employees.

Throughout the book, you will find case studies by current or retired federal employees who offer their view of the federal application process. They will provide you with advice and insight regarding how to write your résumé and cover letter. The case studies can also help you to see what federal hiring managers are looking for when choosing an applicant, as well as common mistakes to avoid. Both federal employees and federal hiring managers will be included in the case studies.

USING THIS BOOK TO GET HIRED BY THE FEDERAL GOVERNMENT

Similarly to being able to recognize an experienced and well-trained salesperson, it is equally easy to identify a bad salesperson. A bad sales associate is ill prepared, unorganized, and unfamiliar with his or her product and consumer. This individual is not remarkable or memorable in a good way and certainly does not inspire people to make big purchases. It is important to imitate the model of the well-trained sales associate, as opposed to the bad sales associate.

This book will give you all the information and resources you will need to sell yourself to a federal employer. You can use this book to walk you through the extensive process of becoming a part of the federal government and reaping the many benefits of your position. A perfectly crafted résumé and cover letter will make a difference when a hiring manager is trying to decide between you and another candidate.

CHAPTER 1

Why Work for the Federal Government

There are a variety of reasons why some people prefer working in the federal government instead of the private sector. To demonstrate some of these reasons, imagine two friends who graduate the same year from the same college. Friend A pursues a job with the federal government and is hired into the Department of Veterans Affairs. A well-respected publishing company hires Friend B.

They each earn several promotions and are able to move up within their respective companies. Friend A has more than 26 days of paid vacation each year, in addition to sick leave, personal days, and ten paid holidays. Friend A has also been allowed to work on a flexible schedule to accommodate his child's schedule. Friend B has 18 days of paid vacation each year, in addition to sick leave and six paid holidays. Friend B requested being put on a flexible schedule, but his bosses decided he was more of an asset in the office. They are each overall happy with their jobs, and their positions within their respective organizations.

Eighteen years after graduating from college, Friend A is planning his retirement and looking into opportunities to join a consulting firm based on his experience in the federal government. Friend B has recently been informed that the company is moving its entire operation overseas, and he will be without a job within eight months. Friend B is now trying to decide on an appropriate career move that will cause the minimal amount of change for his wife and children. Clearly, retirement for Friend B is nowhere in sight.

As you will learn from this chapter, the federal government is not only the largest employer in the United States, but it is also the most dependable. Although some benefits differ from agency to agency, the federal government as a whole offers health and life insurance options that the government partially subsidizes. The opportunities within the federal government far exceed the opportunities available from any other single employer.

THE FEDERAL GOVERNMENT IS A MAJOR EMPLOYER

As of 2008, an estimated 2 million civilians were working for the federal government, not including people who work for the U.S. Postal Service, Central Intelligence Agency, National Security Agency, Defense Intelligence Agency, and National Imagery and Mapping Agency. Except for the U.S. Postal Service, the above agencies are not included in the total count because they do not release specific employment information for security reasons. That number also does not include active military. The U.S. government also employs approximately 35,000 civilians and foreign nationals overseas.

There were 283 agencies within the federal government as of 2009. Of those, 15 are executive cabinet departments, which oversee almost every aspect of life in the United States. There are also smaller independent agencies that employ anywhere from fewer than 100 to several thousand people. The following table shows the number of civilians employed by each of the 15 executive cabinet departments, the judicial branch, the legislative branch, and the top six independent agencies.

Civilian Employment as of November 2008

(Note: This table does not include those employed by the U.S. Postal Service.)

Employer	Civilian Employees in Thousands
Executive Departments	1,664
Defense, total	652
Army	244
Navy	175
Air Force	149
Other	84
Veterans Affairs	280
Homeland Security	171
Justice	108
Treasury	88
Agriculture	82
Interior	67
Health and Human Services	64
Transportation	55
Commerce	39
Labor	16
Energy	15
State	15
Housing and Urban Development	9
Education	4
Judicial Branch	33
Legislative Branch	30
Independent Agencies	180
Social Security Administration	64
National Aeronautics and Space Administration	18
Environmental Protection Agency	18
General Services Administration	12
Office of Personnel Management	5

Employer	Civilian Employees in Thousands
Smithsonian Institution	4
Other	59

Source: U.S. Department of Labor, Bureau of Labor Statistics

These numbers do not include the U.S. Postal Service because the Postal Service became a quasi-independent agency in 1971. The agency has its own job board, which it uses to advertise job openings. It also has its own pay scale, benefits, and rules. As of 2009, the Postal Service employed more than 596,000 people in more than 300 different positions. There are more than 33,000 post offices throughout the country. Although the employee benefits are similar to those of the federal government, postal workers do pay considerably less for health insurance due to union negotiations. Postal workers have the benefits of high starting salaries, flexible work schedules, supplemental work schedules, 401(k)-style Thrift Savings Plans, life insurance, paid holidays, vacation time and sick leave, and generous retirement plans.

The following graphic shows the distribution of federal workers in the United States according to the March 2004 publication "How to get a job in the Federal Government" by the U.S. Department of Labor.

THE RETIREMENT TSUNAMI

The federal government is experiencing what Linda Springer, the former director of the Office of Personnel Management (OPM), coined a "retirement tsunami." According to a 2006 article published in the Washington Post, 60 percent of the federal workforce, or 1.8 million workers, will be ready to retire between 2006 and 2016. As current federal employees are promoted to fill these upper management openings, a large number of jobs will open for new federal employees.

OPM has compiled a list of the ten agencies with the highest percentage of employees who will be eligible for retirement by 2012, which is shown in the following table.

Top Ten Agencies Being Affected by the Retirement Tsunami

Agency	Percentage of employees eligible for retirement by 2012
Federal Aviation Administration	26%
Department of Housing and Urban Development	26%
Social Security Administration	23%
U.S. Department of Education	22%
Department of Energy	22%
National Science Foundation	22%
U.S. General Services Administration	22%
U.S. Department of the Interior	21%
U.S. Department of Labor	21%
Department of the Treasury	21%

Source: FedSmith.com

There is also an increased need for positions considered critical need due to the aging federal workforce. This includes security and law enforcement, nurses, health care workers, and air traffic controllers. Because these positions are considered critical need, the federal government needs to fill these positions prior to them actually being vacant. Law enforcement employees are eligible to retire in less time than other federal positions, which increases the ongoing need for new employees.

THE IMMENSE VARIETY OF JOBS IN THE FEDERAL GOVERNMENT

There are positions available in the federal government for every occupation offered in the private sector. This goes for entry-level maintenance positions to specialized professional positions, such as doctors or engineers. There are jobs for every level of education from an applicant with a high school diploma to an applicant with a Ph.D. There are also jobs for every skill set and trade. Federal agencies run every aspect of American life, which requires a widely diverse group of employees. The USAJOBS website (**www.usajobs.gov**) allows you to search for open jobs by position due to the immense variety of positions. *The USAJOBS website will be discussed further in Chapter 4.* The following chart lists the top 25 occupations in the federal government according to the March 2004 publication "How to Get a Job in the Federal Government" by the U.S. Department of Labor.

Top 25 Occupational Series in the Federal Government, March 2004

Occupation		Employment
Miscellaneous clerks and assistants		74,380
Miscellaneous administration and program positions		69,185
Information technology management positions		64,209
Safety technicians		50,548
Nurses		49,521
Management and program analysis positions		46,791

Occupation		Employment
Secretaries		40,666
Criminal investigators		39,078
General attorneys		29,132
Social insurance administration positions		27,735
Contact representatives		27,379
Contracting positions, including contract officers and specialists		27,269
Air traffic controllers		23,440
General business and industry positions		23,178
General inspection positions, including investigators and compliance officers		22,613
Medical officers, including doctors		22,400
Human resources management positions		22,067
Electronics engineers		20,490
General engineers		18,903
Tax examining positions		17,653
Engineering technicians		17,474
General biological science positions		15,549
General education and training positions, including instructors and consultants		15,335
Correctional officers		15,060
Budget analysis positions		14,388

Source: U.S. Office of Personnel Management, Central Personnel Data File

The four largest areas of employment in the federal government are management, business and financial occupations; professional occupations; office and administrative support occupations; and service occupations. These four areas of employment make up 88.6 percent of all federal jobs. Management, business, and financial occupations cover a wide range of positions in every agency and department of the federal government. Every agency has management positions, as well as employees to handle their financial department. Positions in management include:

- Correctional institution administrators
- Facility managers
- Housing managers
- Personnel management specialist
- Fish and wildlife refuge managers
- Program managers
- Logistics managers
- Supply managers
- Commissary store managers
- Financial administrators

Positions in business and financial occupations include:

- Accountants
- Auditors
- Internal revenue agents
- Financial institution examiners
- Business and industry specialist
- Import specialist
- Trade specialist
- Budget analyst
- Compliance officers
- Collectors
- Tax examiners

Professional occupations cover positions filled by people with specialized education and are needed in all areas of government. These positions require a higher degree of education. These positions also have a higher starting pay than other types of positions. Having a professional specialization can allow new employees to enter the federal government at a higher level than jobs considered entry level. Professional positions include:

- Physicians
- Surgeons
- Nurses
- Geoscientists
- Engineers, including civil, electrical, mechanical, and aerospace
- Botanists
- Psychiatrists
- Architects
- Dietitians and nutritionists
- Biologists

Office and administrative support occupations assist management and perform tasks such as scheduling appointments, drafting letters and e-mails, maintaining files and financial documents, and following through on orders. The educational and experience levels of these employees vary greatly. Office and administrative support positions include:

- Writers
- Editorial assistants
- Record clerks
- Secretaries
- Administrative assistants

Service occupations are filled by the people who provide a direct service within their agency. For example, protective service workers oversee prisons and provide protection. These employees have a wide variety of educational and employment backgrounds. Law enforcement employees must go through the federal law enforcement academy in addition to the normal pre-employment screening. Service occupations include:

- Criminal investigators
- Police officers

- Border control
- Customs inspectors
- Immigration inspectors
- Alcohol, tobacco, and firearms inspectors

The breakdown of jobs by position in the federal government is different than the breakdown of jobs in the private sector. For example, the single largest percentage of jobs in the federal government (about 33 percent) is in management, business, and financial areas, while the largest percentage of jobs in the private sector (20 percent) is in professional positions. The following table shows the breakdown of positions within the federal government as of 2008. This table does not include employees working for the U.S. Postal Service.

Distribution of Employment Positions Within the Federal Government.

Employment Position	Percent Distribution
Management, business, and financial	33.7%
Professional	33.2%
Office and administrative support	13.5%
Service	8.2%
Installation, maintenance and repair	4.6%
Transportation and material moving	2.9%
Construction and extraction	1.6%
Production	1.5%
Sales and related	0.4%
Farming, fishing, and forestry	0.4%

Source: U.S. Department of Labor, Bureau of Labor Statistics

Same job, different setting

All the jobs offered in the private sector are offered in the federal government, but the setting is clearly different. Jobs in the federal government are far less uncertain than jobs in the private sector. For example, a self-employed psychologist might have some months that are busier than others and deal with a wide range of clients. A psychologist working for the Federal Bureau of Prisons will have consistent work year-round and work with the same types of clients the entire time. The benefits of working for the federal government are as diverse as the positions available. *See Appendix G for a listing of federal job titles by college major.*

In addition to the elimination of unreliable variables, the federal government is highly structured in a mechanistic structure, while many private sector employers operate under a more organic structure. In mechanistic structures, there is a clear and recognized chain of command. There are also policies and procedures for everything, which must be followed. Promotions move along the chain of command, and employees do not skip levels of command while being promoted. Organic structures are based more around team projects and peer-reviewed work. The following table shows the basic organization of the federal government.

Organization of the Federal Government

Legislative Branch	Executive Branch	Judicial Branch
Senate	President	U.S. Supreme Court
House of Representatives	Executive Office of the President	U.S. Court of Appeals
Architect of the Capitol	Department of Agriculture	Court International Trade
Congressional Budget Office	Department of Commerce	U.S. Tax Court
General Accounting Office	Department of Defense	Court of Military Appeals
Government Accountability Office	Department of Education	Federal Judicial Center
Government Printing Office	Department of Energy	Sentencing Commission
Library of Congress	Department of Health and Human Services	
	Department of Housing and Urban Development	

Legislative Branch	Executive Branch	Judicial Branch
	Department of Interior	
	Department of Justice	
	Department of Labor	
	Department of State	
	Department of Transportation	
	Department of Treasury	
	Department of Veterans Affairs	

Source: Washburn University School of Law

BENEFITS OF WORKING FOR THE FEDERAL GOVERNMENT

The benefits of working for the federal government include the job benefits, but also the benefits and opportunities that an employee receives as a result of working for the federal government. The benefits and opportunities include the opportunity to travel, relocate, and transfer from one agency to another without the transfer affecting your retirement. There are also the intangible benefits of working for the federal government, such as being a part of an organization that serves the American people and making a difference in the lives of others. The job benefits offered by the federal government are family-friendly and allow employees to not have to choose between family and career.

> "Working for the federal government is about more than money. People grow up dreaming about working for NASA or the CIA or becoming a park ranger or cancer researcher. We should be applauding these hard-working civil servants."
>
> **- John Berry, director, United States Office of Personnel Management**

The medical benefits offered by the federal government are highly rated. Employees can accumulate up to 13 sick days each year. There are approximately 180 health plans to chose from, so employees can choose the plan that best fits their situation. Federal employees also have the availability to choose dental and vision insurance. Part of the premiums and out-of-pocket expenses can be paid with pre-tax money using flexible spending accounts.

All federal employees can earn up to 26 vacation days each year based on their length of employment, and they can carry up to 30 vacation days from one year to the next. Federal workers also get ten paid holidays each year. Obviously, all federal employees cannot get the day off on each holiday because not all agencies can completely shut down. In that situation, employees who work on paid holidays either get an alternate day off, or they are paid double for eight hours to compensate for having to work. Although the amount of flexibility in the schedule varies from agency to agency, many federal jobs provide opportunities for employees to have flexible work schedules or the opportunity to work from home. Depending on the agency, the federal government also provides their employees with child care and elder care resources, child support assistance, and job-sharing positions.

Paid holidays

All federal employees receive ten paid holidays each year. Obviously, not all federal employees can take off on each of the ten holidays. Each department will rotate who works which holiday to ensure that all employees get some holidays off, and employees who must work on one of the ten holidays will receive holiday pay. The ten paid holidays for federal employees are:

1. New Year's Day
2. Martin Luther King Jr.'s Birthday
3. President's Birthday
4. Memorial Day
5. Independence Day
6. Labor Day
7. Columbus Day
8. Veterans Day
9. Thanksgiving Day
10. Christmas Day

Family and Medical Leave Act

The Family and Medical Leave Act (FMLA) was passed in 1993 and allows up to 12 weeks of unpaid, job-protected leave per year for employees who work for a public agency, public or private elementary or secondary school, or a company with more than 50 employees. The job-protected leave is permitted in four specific situations:

1. The birth and care of a newborn child
2. The placement of a child with the employee for adoption or foster care
3. To care for an immediate family member (spouse, child, or parent) who has a serious medical condition
4. When the employee has a serious medical condition and is unable to work

In June 2010, the U.S. Department of Labor announced a clarification to the definition of "son and daughter" under FMLA. Formerly, under this act, "child" was defined as one related either biologically or legally. The new definition of child will include any child an employee has taken responsibility for and for whom the employee assumes the role of caregiver. This will extend family-leave rights to grandparents raising their grandchildren, relatives caring for children while the child's parent is called to active military duty, and employees caring for the children of a same-sex partner. Because all federal employees are part of a public agency, they are all able to benefit from this change.

Retirement benefits

The federal government has a three-part retirement program, which includes social security, a 401(k)-style plan, and benefits based on years of service with the government and salary history. Because retirement is based on years of service instead of age, federal employees have the opportunity to retire at a younger age than private-sector employees who must rely on only social security or social security and a 401(k). For example, law enforcement employees are able to retire after 25 years regardless of age or after 20 years and age 50 years. A very important aspect of the federal retirement program is that federal employees get lifetime health insurance. Federal employees are also provided with life insurance and long-term care insurance.

Pay for federal workers

Federal workers are paid based on what they call a grade scale. Every position has a specifically designated grade. There are 15 grades, and each grade has 10 steps. The grade designated for a specific position is based on the education and/or experience required to work in that position. The higher the grade for a position is the higher the salary. The steps represent promotions or raises within a grade. For example, you may have a GS-10 position, which is equivalent to having an advanced degree or equal experience. A GS-10 can make from $45,095 per year and $58,622 per year. Within GS-10, each step increase is equal to a $1503 pay raise.

GS Levels by Education	
GS-1	No high school diploma
GS-2 (GS-3 for clerk-steno positions)	High school diploma
GS-3	1 year of full-time study after high school
GS-4	Associate degree or 2 years of full-time study after high school
GS-5 or GS-7 (depending on agency policy and applicant's academic credentials)	Bachelor's degree or 4 years of full-time study after high school
GS-7	Bachelor's degree plus 1 year of full-time graduate study
GS-9 (GS-11 for some research positions)	Master's degree or 2 years of full-time graduate study
GS-9	Law degree (J.D. or LL.B.)
GS-11 (GS-12 for some research positions)	Ph.D. or equivalent doctorate or advanced law degree (LL.M.)

Source: U.S. Office of Personal Management

On average, the pay for federal jobs is higher than jobs in the private sector, and the federal government provides locality pay, which means the wage reflects the region where the job is located. This means jobs located in areas with a higher cost of living pay higher than jobs located in an area with a lower cost of living. Locality pay can change if after being hired as a federal employee you transfer or are promoted to another position in a different region. Locality pay is particularly important for federal employees because the amount of money an employee receives upon retirement is based on the salary they were receiving at the time of retirement. This means an employee can transfer to a region with a higher locality pay prior to retiring as a means of boosting their retirement. The following table provides an example of the difference in locality pay. Each amount shown in the second column reflects the starting pay for a GS-7 position, which is equivalent to a position requiring a bachelor's degree or equivalent experience. The first listing on the table is the general schedule — the starting pay for a GS-7 position in regions that do not have locality pay.

GS-7 2010 Locality Pay

Location	GS-7 Starting Salary
General Schedule	$33,979
Atlanta, GA	$40,534
Boston, MA	$42,406
Chicago, IL	$42,508
Denver, CO	$41,631
Detroit, MI	$42,165
Huntsville, AL	$39,422
Los Angeles, CA	$43,208
Miami, FL	$41,043
New York, NY	$43,738
Phoenix, AZ	$39,674

Source: U.S. Office of Personal Management

Federal employees also receive Sunday pay and night differential pay. Sunday pay is compensation employees receive when they must work a Sunday shift; they are paid 25 percent more of their base pay per hour. If their base pay is $20 an hour, their Sunday pay will be $25 an hour. Employees who work between 6 p.m. and 6 a.m. or who are asked to work overtime at night receive night pay. Employees who work between 6 p.m. and 6 a.m. receive 10 percent of the base pay more per hour. Once again, if their base pay is $20 an hour, their night differential pay will be $22 an hour.

The federal government promotes from within whenever there is a qualified internal candidate. This provides new employees who are hard working and motivated the opportunity to quickly move up within their agency. Because the opportunities for promotions are for an entire agency, an employee can be promoted and move to a different location if a higher position is not available at their current location. Employees are also provided with on-the-job training, employee development programs, and certification opportunities.

Federal employees are granted recruitment incentives, relocation incentives, and incentive rewards for hard-to-fill positions. Employees have the opportunity to relocate through interagency transfers and can choose to jump agencies if an ideal position opens in a different federal agency. Although not all agencies do, some federal agencies have the option of offering student loan repayment to their employees. All federal employees also get a cost-of-living adjustment (COLA) to their pay every year.

Working for the federal government gives most employees a sense of purpose in their job. According to the U.S. Merit Systems Protection Board's *Merit Principles Survey 2005*, 95 percent of respondents stated that they felt their agency's mission was vitally important, 92 percent of respondents understood how their specific position contributed to the overall mission of the agency, and 88 percent believed their work was meaningful. This sense of purpose and meaningfulness increases employees' overall satisfaction with their jobs and makes them more productive workers.

The federal government also demonstrates a desire to take care of their employees through the passage of disaster assistance programs and Employee Assistance Programs (EAP). These programs are designed to help federal workers and their families affected by natural disasters. For example, in the wake of Hurricane Katrina, federal workers affected by the hurricane were provided with counseling and generous time off work to deal with housing, family, and health issues that came about as a result of the hurricane.

IF YOU ARE LOOKING FOR JOB STABILITY, FEDERAL JOBS ARE FOR YOU

One of the greatest benefits of working for the federal government is job security. Although positions might be eliminated at the federal level, the federal government works to provide displaced workers with another position. The Interagency Career Transition Assistance Plan (ICTAP) is a program designed to offer displaced federal employees priority when applying for a position in a federal agency other than the agency for which they formerly worked. In addition to rarely being laid off, it is extremely difficult for a federal employee to be fired. The firing process for poor performance in the federal government is very cumbersome and can take more than a year. Even after being fired, a federal employee has several chances to appeal the decision. Paul Light, a professor of public service at New York University and expert on federal employment, points out that out of the entire federal government, only a couple hundred employees are fired for poor performance each year.

Presidential Memorandum
Presidential POWER Initiative: Protecting Our Workers and Ensuring Reemployment
July 19, 2010

According to workers' compensation reports, federal employees made over 79,000 new injury claims in 2009. Many of these work-related injuries have been determined to be preventable according to investigation reports. President Obama has determined that agencies and departments should be doing more to protect their workers from injury and work-related illnesses. For this reason, President Obama has established the Protecting Our Workers and Ensuring Reemployment (POWER) initiative. This initiative will be active from 2011 to 2014, which is when its effectiveness will be evaluated and its future will be determined.

The POWER initiative will set higher standards in workplace safety, which each agency will be responsible for maintaining. In addition to higher performance targets, the POWER initiative will also create a system to collect and analyze data regarding work-related injuries and illnesses. This analysis will allow agencies to create safety and health management programs, which will fit the unique needs of their agency. The safety and health management programs will be based on methods and techniques that have already been proven successful in the past.

The POWER initiative will be lead by the Secretary of Labor and will work toward the following goals:

- Reduce the total number of injury and illness cases
- Reduce the amount of time lost due to injury and illness
- Analyze lost time data for injuries and illnesses
- Increase the timeliness of filing workers' compensation claims
- Increase the timeliness of filing wage-loss claims
- Reduce lost production day rates
- Speed up employees' return to work after injury or illness cases

Positions will not be shipped abroad

It is difficult to say exactly how many Americans have lost their jobs to out-sourcing, as employers are not required to keep records of those numbers. The practice started after U.S. companies found it was cheaper to have work done in other countries — where wages are significantly lower — than to pay for the same jobs to be done by an American worker. Several studies have been conducted in an attempt to get a picture of the size of the problem.

In 2001, Cornell and the University of Massachusetts found that more than 201,000 jobs had been outsourced that year. During the same period, unionized jobs dropped by 39 percent while non-unionized production jobs dropped by 29 percent. Many of the positions outsourced were white collar or information technology (IT) positions. According to a 2009 study by AMR Research, Inc., 80 percent of enterprises plan to increase or maintain their current IT outsourcing. Finally, in 2002 the Forrester Research Group estimated that 3.3 million U.S. jobs would be moved to India, China, and Russia by 2017.

Ironically, the positions being outsourced the most in the private sector, IT positions, are those most aggressively recruited by the federal government. IT professionals, especially those who specialize in cyber security, receive higher pay than private sector IT professionals, and they might be eligible for recruitment bonuses. Federal positions are not outsourced to other countries, so employees never need to fear being laid off for this reason. Most federal positions are location specific, so employees can choose never to relocate. Additionally, the federal government recognizes the value of experienced and highly qualified employees, so older employees do not need to fear being laid off or forced into retirement only to be replaced by younger, less expensive workers.

Work for the federal government must go on — no matter what

Another source of job security is the fact that federal jobs are critical to the running of the country. Federal agencies cannot be shut down like private businesses can. The function of these agencies cannot be substituted or abandoned without detrimental effects. The federal government keeps running regardless of what is going on in the economy. In fact, a bad economy, natural disasters, and other national emergencies actually increase the need for federal employees. In addition, federal employees do not get their benefits cut or their retirement reduced as a result of budget cuts.

CASE STUDY:
FEDERAL EMPLOYMENT
EQUALS JOB SECURITY

Matt Harkins
Transportation security officer
U.S. Department of Transportation

I was attracted to a position with the federal government because of the job stability. Following college, I got my first job working for a construction company, but I was laid off a year later. I quickly got a new job, but that company went bankrupt just a few months after hiring me. I had

been at my third job for 18 months when it downsized.
third job that someone recommended I check out the US,
I still was not specifically looking for a job with the federal government, at
that point, I was looking for any job that would enable me to pay the bills.

I found the USAJOBS website easy to navigate and full of helpful information. I used the résumé builder to create a new résumé, which I
appreciated very much. Writing was never one of my strong points, and
I was always concerned about what potential employers thought of the
résumé I had created. Although I was still out of work for close to a year,
I finally landed a job with the U.S. Department of Transportation, which
is where I have worked for the past six years.

I would absolutely recommend the federal government as a potential
employer for recent college grads. I wasted almost four years in jobs that
were completely controlled by the economy, which resulted in a complete lack of job stability. I was surprised by the wide variety of benefits
offered to me as a new employee. All the other jobs I had offered benefits progressively based on the amount of time the employee had been
there. For example, my first two jobs did not offer any vacation time until
after you had been there for a year.

I also highly recommend the USAJOBS résumé builder. Even with this
program, it still takes time and effort to create your résumé, but it was a
relief to not have to try to figure out the spacing. I also did not have to
sit forever trying to think about what I should add in my résumé. I just
followed the sections provided.

A TOUGH ECONOMY CAN MEAN EXPANSION OF FEDERAL JOBS

Not only will the government not shut down when the economy is bad, but
also a tough economy often provides more federal job opportunities by expanding departments and agencies. In an effort to create jobs, the government has a history of initiating special projects. The New Deal enacted by
President Roosevelt during the Great Depression is a prime example of this
practice. President Roosevelt created several new agencies, including, but

ot limited to, the Social Security Act (SSA), Fair Employment Act (FEA), Securities and Exchange Commission (SEC), Tennessee Valley Authority (TVA), and National Labor Relations Board (NLRB). The numerous new agencies became referred to as alphabet agencies. The agencies created by the New Deal increased jobs and completed projects related to issues such as infrastructure. In 2009, the Obama administration passed the Recovery Act in an effort to increase employment opportunities in a similar fashion.

The Recovery Act and new government jobs

Versions of the Recovery Act were introduced in both the House of Representatives and the Senate in January of 2009. The house version of the bill was introduced on January 26 and passed by a 244 to 188 vote by January 28. The Senate version of the bill was introduced on January 6 and passed by a 61 to 37 vote on February 10. President Obama signed the act into law by on February 17. The act includes tax cuts and increases social welfare programs, as well as federal spending on education, health care, and infrastructure.

In passing the Recovery Act, President Obama and Congress had three goals in mind. The first goal was to create new jobs and save existing ones. The second goal was to encourage economic activity and invest in long-term growth, and the third goal was to encourage accountability and transparency in government spending. According to the act, the government will achieve its goals by providing $288 billion in tax cuts and benefits for working families and small businesses. Federal funds for education and health care will increase. There will be approximately $275 billion in federal contracts, grants, and loans. The only stipulation is that recipients of funds are required to report their spending. This allows the federal government to track the recovery funds and to ensure they are used appropriately.

The Recovery Act has led to a dramatic increase in the availability of federal jobs, as well as private sector jobs. The increase in federal jobs is due in part to an increase in agency responsibilities and partly to the increase of projects funded by the Recovery Act. According to the USAJOBS website, as of May 2010 there are 56 federal agencies hiring additional employees due to the Recovery Act. The following agencies were allocated increased funding under the Recovery Act: Federal Transit Administration, Environmental Protection Agency, U.S. Army Corps of Engineers, U.S. General Services Administration, Department of Housing and Urban Development, Bureau of Reclamation, National Park Service, U.S. Forest Service, Bureau of Indians Affairs, Natural Resources Conservation Service, Bureau of Land Management, National Wildlife Refuge System, National Fish Hatchery System, International Boundary and Water Commission, Social Security Administration, U.S. Department of State, and Farm Service Agency.

WHY GETTING A FEDERAL JOB MIGHT BE TOUGHER THAN A PRIVATE SECTOR POSITION

Despite the fact that the federal government is the country's largest employer, federal positions are highly competitive. The federal government offers great jobs with great pay and even greater benefits, and it can afford to be picky when selecting employees. The following table shows a sampling of five different positions and the mean pay for that position in the private sector versus the mean pay for that position in the federal government. This means there are multiple qualified people applying for the jobs. The number of applicants can range from less than 12 to several hundred depending on the position and location. Each applicant will need to rely on the strength of his or her résumé and cover letter to stand out among the rest.

Federal Pay versus Private Sector Pay

	Federal government	Private sector
Budget analyst	$76,480	$69,240
Social worker	$67,830	$50,470
Correctional officer	$52,310	$42,610
Forester	$62,200	$55,220
Transportation, storage, and distribution managers	$94,860	$85,470

Source: Bureau of Labor Statistics, Information from May 2009

The qualifications for federal jobs are specific and detailed. An applicant not following application directions or not providing all the required credentials will be eliminated from the pool of applicants for the position. An omission of the required credentials will lead to an applicant's résumé being thrown out of the pile regardless of whether he or she actually has the needed credentials. The hiring process for federal jobs is longer and more extensive than the hiring process for private sector jobs. This can make it difficult for applicants who are looking for immediate employment. Although some agencies still allow applicants to submit their résumés and cover letters through the mail or by fax, many agencies are moving to a completely electronic application process. However, there is always a mail-in option in order not to exclude applicants without Internet access. Taking the mail-in option will require accessing the needed forms, including an extensive questionnaire, and sending it along with your résumé, cover letter, and credentials.

The job search process for federal jobs is not difficult, but does require specific information. An applicant unfamiliar with the OPM website or the USAJOBS website might have difficulty finding the right position to apply for. *The OPM website will be discussed in detail in Chapter 2, and the USAJOBS website will be discussed in Chapter 4.* Both websites are very important in the federal hiring process.

Standards and rules are sometimes different

One of the many reasons it is vitally important to carefully read the job description is to know exactly what the hiring manager requires. Some federal positions require the completion of a written exam. Some positions require a physical fitness test in order to qualify. The standards set for federal employees to verify their qualifications are sometimes different and often stricter than the standards set in the private sector. For example, if a federal job has a physical fitness or ability to lift requirement, the applicant will need to demonstrate they meet that requirement. Hiring managers in the private sector are more likely to accept an applicant's word as the truth to avoid the time and energy of getting all the applicant's information verified. The federal government has the resources and work force to verify everything submitted to them by an applicant.

Exceptions to the federal rules

How to get a job in the federal government
U.S. Department of Labor
Bureau of Labor Statistics

A few agencies and occupations are exempt from some standard regulations that govern federal hiring in the civil service. Jobs in those agencies and occupations do not have to be listed on the USAJOBS website. And people who apply for those jobs might have to fill out different application forms or follow different procedures than those described in this book.

Excepted-service agencies include those in the legislative and judicial branches of government and several agencies in the executive branch, including the U.S. Postal Service, the Federal Bureau of Investigation, and the intelligence services. A few occupations, such as attorneys and Foreign Service workers, also are exempt from some of the procedures described here, and so are positions that last fewer than 180 days.

Even when they do not have to, many excepted-service agencies still follow the standard procedures. These agencies often list openings on the USAJOBS website, for example, and require the same information in applications and résumés. Contact excepted-service agencies to be sure of their hiring methods.

Finally, a small percentage of positions in the federal government are set aside for political appointees. Elected officials appoint people to these jobs.

Does "who you know" matter?

Although all applicants have to go through the same application process for individual positions, having the right references or people pulling for you can make a difference.

According to the U.S. Merit Systems Protection Board's *In Search of Highly Skilled Workers; a Study in the Hiring of Upper Level employees from Outside the Federal Government*, February 2008, 45 percent of new employees learned about the job through a personal contact. Obviously, a friend or relative will not be able to get you the job. However, if he or she works within the agency you are applying for, he or she can put in a recommendation to the hiring manager on your behalf. Networking is an important part of all federal positions and will help a federal employee understand the ins and outs of their agency faster. Once in the federal government, networking will also help in obtaining promotions.

How a perfect résumé and cover letter might even the odds

According to the U.S. Merit Systems Protection Board report, when questioned as to why they chose the candidate they did, 68 percent of hiring managers cited their main reason as being, "This particular applicant was clearly better qualified than the others, including internal applicants." This shows that applicants are judged based on their qualifications. Determining an individual as best qualified includes taking into consideration the quality of his or her résumé and cover letter. At the beginning stages of the application process, the résumé and cover letter are going to be the only items representing you to the hiring manager. Providing a perfect résumé and cover letter will show the hiring manager your ability to communicate through writing, your organizational skills, your attention to detail, and your professionalism.

Sixty-four percent of hiring managers also cited "to fill a skill gap" as their reason for choosing the applicant they chose to fill the position. The major duties section of the job description will list all the tasks the applicant will be expected to perform if hired. Any information an applicant can provide about knowledge or experience in regard to the major duties will increase his or her chances of being hired. For example, having experience in a specific computer program used by the agency might mean the applicant can "fill a skill gap." This is why it is vitally important to properly represent yourself in your résumé and cover letter. You are the sales associate and the hiring manager is the consumer. Your résumé and cover letter should sell you to the hiring manger by highlighting all your skills and accomplishments.

Using the government's methods

The USAJOBS website provides a tool called a résumé builder. This program will walk applicants through the résumé creating process. The major benefit of using this program is that it provides prompts for all the needed information, so an applicant is less likely to forget to include information in the résumé. USAJOBS' résumé builder also has a built-in spell check and word count. Each section of a federal application and résumé has a specific allowed word count. Going over the allowed word count can result in the application being discarded. Although using the résumé builder is not required, it is a valuable tool that can help you in your application process.

The USAJOBS website also allows applicants to apply for most positions online through the website. This streamlines the process, and applicants only need to follow the steps provided by the website. Not all positions request or require applicants to submit their résumés online. There are open positions on the USAJOBS website that request the application packages be sent through the mail or faxed. It is important to follow the instructions on how to apply provided in the job description. Once again, using this tool will ensure that no information is forgotten. At the end of each job description, the hiring manger's contact information is provided. Applicants should keep that information for future reference.

What the federal government is looking for in its candidates

The federal government wants well-qualified candidates to fill all its positions. Regardless of whether the position is for a maintenance worker or a surgeon, the résumé and cover letter will determine for the hiring manager whether the applicant is qualified for the position. Every portion of the résumé and cover letter should be completed with the highest level of attention to detail. An applicant does not know exactly what will stand out to the hiring manager, so every portion should be treated as if it were the most important section.

When hiring managers are reviewing résumés and cover letters, they should be able to identify an applicant's most relevant and important experience quickly. Although it is acceptable for résumés to be longer than one page, they should not contain information that is not essential for the hiring manager to know. Hiring managers are very busy, and if they are not drawn into reading a résumé, they will be more likely to skim over most of it and move on to the next applicant's packet.

Executive Order
Increasing Federal Employment of Individuals with Disabilities
July 26, 2010

Currently, individuals with disabilities only represent approximately 5 percent of the 2.5 million federal workers. Further, individuals with targeted disabilities represent less than 1 percent of the total workforce. Currently, targeted disabilities are defined as "set forth on the form for self identification of disability," according to OPM. However, by the end of 2011, OPM will be reviewing the effectiveness of this definition and possibly updating or revising it.

With these numbers in mind, President Obama has reviewed Executive Order 13163, which was put in place on July 26, 2000 by former President Bill Clinton. President Clinton's order called for an additional 100,000 individuals with disabilities to be hired in to the Federal workforce over a five-year period. However, less than six months later, President Clinton left office, and no steps were taken to fulfill this order. President Obama has created an updated revision of this order with steps toward increasing the employment of individuals with disabilities. The order is divided into two basic sections designed to create a plan to increase employment of individuals with disabilities and retain current individuals with disabilities. The details of the plan include:

1. Within 60 days of this executive order, several departments will work together to create a model of recruitment and hiring strategies, which can be implemented in agencies and departments needing to increase their number of individuals with disabilities. The departments involved in the creation of these strategies will also create a mandatory training program for human resources personnel and hiring managers on the employment of individuals with disabilities.

2. Within 120 days of the above strategies and programs being created, every agency will use them to create an agency-specific plan of action to promote and increase their employment of individuals
with disabilities.

3. Each agency will provide a senior-level official to be responsible for the successful implementation of the plan and for increasing their employment opportunities for individuals with disabilities. Part of this responsibility will include coordinating employment counseling to match perspective employees with disabilities to employment needs within the agency.

4. Agencies will also utilize the federal government's Schedule A excepted service hiring authority in order to increase participation of individuals with disabilities in the internship, fellowship, and training and mentoring programs.

5. OPM will make itself available to any agency needing assistance through this process. OPM will also compile and post government-wide statistics in the employment of individuals with disabilities.

Increasing Agencies' Retention and Return to Work of Individuals with Disabilities

The second part of the executive order deals with improving the ways in which agencies accommodate and retain current employees with disabilities. The details of this plan include:

1. Any agency that has been targeted as having difficulty retaining the employment of individuals with disabilities will receive assistance from OPM, as well as other department heads. This assistance may include increased and targeted training, increased funds, and increased access to specialized technology.

2. In order to increase the return to work rate of individuals with disabilities, which resulted from a work-related injury, agencies will increase the availability of job accommodations, as well as light and limited duty jobs.

A PERFECTLY CRAFTED RÉSUMÉ AND COVER LETTER COULD GET YOU THE JOB

The purpose of this book is to help you create the perfect résumé and cover letter because those are the key to potential employment. The information you decide to include in your résumé is as important as how you present that information. Candidates who do not take the time to perfectly craft their résumé and cover letter are unlikely to be noticed. Your résumé and cover letter will not only demonstrate your writing ability, but also the seriousness of your intentions. Taking time to make sure your résumé and cover letter are perfect will demonstrate your desire for federal employment.

You need to think of your résumé and cover letter as your one chance to sell the most important product you have: yourself. Your goal is to leave the hiring manager wanting to meet you after reading your information. The hiring manager should be impressed with your presentation and professionalism. The next chapter will provide you will all the information you will need to know prior to starting your job search.

CHAPTER 2

Information to Know Before Creating Your Résumé and Cover Letter

When working on a project around the house, "measure twice and cut once" is a good axiom to follow. Once you make the cut, there is no going back. A mistake when cutting means having to start over from the beginning. It wastes time and money if new materials are needed. It also causes frustration and stress. Measuring twice before making a cut enables you to be ready and prepared. There will be significantly fewer mistakes and time needed to complete the project.

This rule also applies to looking for federal jobs. The more you know about the agency and position to which you are applying, the less time you will waste while preparing your résumé and cover letter. Each job description provides all the information needed to apply for that particular position. Reading over the job description carefully will prevent you from wasting time preparing for a position you are not qualified for, and it will allow you to tailor your résumé and cover letter to fit the position. Double-checking the information you have compiled will also prevent you from realizing after the application packet has been sent that you forgot an important credential or prepared a form incorrectly.

WHAT THE FEDERAL GOVERNMENT IS LOOKING FOR IN ITS CANDIDATES

The federal government is looking for applicants who are qualified for every position it is looking to fill. Hiring managers for the federal government will relist a position to attract more applicants before they will hire someone who is not qualified according to the standards listed in the job description.

Although education is very important, experienced related to the position is regarded more favorably than anything else. Accurately explaining past experience, particularly in regards to the qualifications for the position will make an applicant more appealing to a hiring manager.

Your résumé and cover letter are very important because they will provide the hiring manager with all the information he or she needs to determine if you are qualified. If there is information missing from your résumé, it is not organized, or it is hard to read, your application package might be discarded, despite the fact you are highly qualified for the position. Another common mistake that can negatively affect an applicant's eligibility is submitting a résumé and cover letter that is generic and that does not specifically address the position for which you are applying.

Taking note of the requirements and qualifications listed in the job description

Every job description will list key requirements and qualifications. The key requirements will be the most basic qualifications for the job and items that will be required prior and during employment. For example, some jobs require a background check, random drug tests, a physical exam, or the ability to travel. The key requirements might also cover information that is important for the applicant to know prior to applying. The following are examples of information included in the key requirements section of the job description from job descriptions listed on the USAJOBS website:

Example 1: Travel and relocation expenses will not be paid

Example 2: Knowledge and understanding of the decontamination/sterilization process

The key requirements include essential information about the position and are one of the first things you should read in the job description. If you do not meet the key requirements, then you are not qualified for the position and should continue your job search.

The qualifications are more extensive and cover the key requirements, plus other qualifications, such as education, certifications, and experience. An important aspect of the qualifications section is the number of years of experience listed in the job description. For example, a job posting might require one year of experience in a supervisory position. The federal government will accept partial time in a different position. Going back to the previous example, if an applicant had a position that was not a supervisory position, but they held a supervisory position during specific periods, the applicant can add those periods of time. So, if the applicant was promoted to a supervisory position six months earlier, but during the three years prior to being promoted, the applicant had spent a combined total of six months filling in as a temporary supervisor while two other supervisors were out on maternity leave, they have a total of one year in a supervisory position.

When highlighting how an applicant fits the qualifications for the position in his or her résumé and cover letter, the applicant should be as specific as possible. An applicant should provide exact information on how much time he or she spent in a past position, his or her major responsibilities, the number of people being supervised, the size of the operation, and the money value of the product being sold. These types of specific examples will provide the hiring manager with concrete examples of the applicant's professional abilities. *The use of specific numbers and amounts will be covered more extensively in Chapter 7.*

Know which job you are applying for

The first thing you want to look at when checking job descriptions is the position title. Job titles in the federal government might be different than job titles in the private sector. For example, administrative assistant jobs in the federal government are titled based on the agency and department for which the position is under. Instead of listing the job under administrative assistant, it might be listed as human resources assistance. If you are unsure about the position title, the USAJOBS website allows job seekers to search by agency and pay grade. Searching by agency will allow you to narrow your search to only agencies for which you know you want to work. Knowing the specific agency will also help you to understand the position better. For example, law enforcement in a federal prison is different than law enforcement working for Homeland Security. Although you will still need to study the job description to understand what the position entails, knowing the agency will help in the initial search. Pay grade will also help you search for the right position because the pay grade directly correlates to the level of education and experience the hiring manager is looking for in an applicant. You can narrow your search by pay grade depending on your level of education. Reading the job summary will also help job seekers define the position.

Another thing to keep in mind is where the job might lead. For example, if you are looking to get into the Federal Bureau of Prisons, it is not likely that you will be hired in as a department manager or senior caseworker, regardless of the amount of education you have. However, you can be hired in as a correctional officer and then actively pursue promotional opportunities. The federal government is always eager to promote from within the group of employees who already work for the government.

The job description will also include a general description of the position, a section titled "Major Duties," and a section called "How You Will Be

Evaluated." The general description will provide the name of the position, the location, and the agency doing the hiring. These are all important factors to consider. The location of the position is important because you do not know how long you will need to stay in that location. Although there are always opportunities for promotions and lateral moves that involve relocation, these are also competitive, and you will not have any guarantees going into a position. The agency is also important to consider. Believing in the mission of the agency is an important element of job satisfaction. Unlike private sector jobs, federal jobs are serving the nation, and every job has a very specific goal and role within the government system.

The "Major Duties" section is very important because it will detail all the duties of the position. You should only apply for the position if you are confident you can fulfill all the duties listed in this section. In an interview, the hiring manager will ask questions regarding the major duties of the position to ensure that they can be successfully completed. The following is an example of items listed in the "Major Duties" section of a job posting found on the USAJOBS website:

> **Example 1:** Primary responsibilities will be to coordinate clinical experiences and teaching nurse practitioner students in the clinical setting.

> **Example 2:** Necessary skills include excellent interpersonal and organization skills and the ability to collaborate with a variety of health care staff and affiliate nursing programs.

An applicant for this position should be confident in these skills and in his or her ability to fulfill the major duties of this position. The applicant's résumé and cover letter should highlight past experiences, work history, and education that will demonstrate his or her ability to fulfill the major duties. You can use the information and keywords in this section when crafting your résumé and cover letter.

The section titled "How You Will Be Evaluated" is also very important because it details how the hiring manager will evaluate each applicant. Applicants should pay careful attention to what the hiring manager will be looking at when making a hiring decision. However, even if a résumé and cover letter are not listed in this section, but required as part of your application package, the résumé and cover letter are still very important and can make a difference. The following are two examples of this section pulled from job ads listed on the USAJOBS website:

> **Example 1:** Your résumé and/or supporting documentation will be verified. Please follow all instructions carefully. Errors or omissions might affect your rating or consideration for employment.

> **Example 2:** To determine if you are qualified for this job, a review of your résumé and supporting documents will be made and compared against your responses to the assessment questionnaire. The numeric rating you receive is based on your responses to the questionnaire. The score is a measure of the degree to which your background matches the knowledge, skills, and abilities required of this position.

Each of these examples makes specific reference to the résumé and supporting documents. Example 1 emphasizes the importance of reading the instructions carefully and paying close attention to what is included in the résumé and cover letter. Example 2 gives a little more information regarding how the applicant will be evaluated, but it still goes back to the accuracy of the résumé and cover letter.

Apply only to the positions you are qualified for

Applying for a position for which you are not qualified will only waste your time and the time of the hiring manager reviewing the application packages. Knowing if you qualify for a position is as easy as carefully reading the job description. When a job announcement closes, all the applications will be reviewed. Those applicants who did not include all the necessary information or follow the application instructions exactly are discarded. The remaining applications are then reviewed, and the best qualified (BQ) list is created. The applicants who make the BQ list are the ones who will be contacted for further information or an interview.

Trying to get a federal job does not need to resemble fishing with a net. This is often referred to as the mass-mailing technique. This refers to when an applicant writes a generic résumé and cover letter and then mails it out to several departments for several different positions. Hiring managers will immediately recognize a generically written résumé and cover letter. Not tailoring a résumé and cover letter to the specific job is one way to prevent you from making the BQ list. Instead of applying for many jobs and hoping something will come through, read the job descriptions carefully, and apply for the ones for which you are completely qualified.

Knowing the ins and outs of the job is a must when it comes to designing your résumé and cover letter

Knowing the ins and outs of the job will enable you to tailor your résumé to the position for which you are applying. Although it is important not to lie or exaggerate, you can highlight the portions of your education and experience that directly apply to the position. Print the job description from your computer. Once you have a hard copy, go through the key requirements, qualifications, and major duties sections, and highlight keywords and phrases. These are the words and phrases used to describe the qualities the hiring manager will be looking for in an applicant. *How to identify and implement keywords and phrases is covered extensively in Chapter 5 of this book.* It is important to remember when writing your résumé to demonstrate a wide range of skills and experiences that directly apply to the position.

Citizenship and other minimum requirements

There are actually very few minimum requirements across the board. Applicants do need to be U.S. citizens for most positions. They also must be either 18 years old or 16 years old and have graduated high school, earned the certificate equivalent to graduating, completed a formal vocational training program, received a statement from school authorities agreeing with their preference for employment rather than education, or be currently enrolled in college or a vocational program. Some programs have higher age requirements, such as law enforcement agencies that might require applicants to be old enough to use a firearm.

Some positions state a maximum age for applicants. For example, law enforcement positions have a maximum applicant age of between 34 and 37. The maximum age does vary from agency to agency. Law enforcement jobs cover more than just police, correctional officers, and marshal positions, so it is important to know if the position you are applying for is considered law enforcement.

Education requirements also vary by position. *Education requirements will be covered more extensively later in this chapter.* It is important to note, however, that the federal government will look at work history and experience in place of formal education. For example, if the job description states, "master's degree or equivalent experience" in the key requirements or qualifications sections, this means they will consider an applicant without a master's degree if that applicant has comparable work experience.

There is also an absence of an all-inclusive rule against ex-offenders working for the federal government, which means ex-offenders should not hesitate from seeking a position with the federal government. If an applicant has a criminal record, he or she is required to be completely honest about the nature of the crime and the conviction. If the applicant is dishonest regarding his or her criminal history, whether by lying or omitting information, he or she risks the application being discarded. There are some positions an ex-offender cannot fulfill. For example, according to the Omnibus Consolidated Appropriations Act of 1997, individuals convicted of a misdemeanor for domestic violence are "prohibited from employment in any position requiring the individual: to ship, transport, possess, or receive firearms or ammunition." If you have any questions regarding your criminal history, you should contact the hiring manager for the position in which you are applying.

Credentials are important

Credentials refer to all the supporting information and documents an applicant must include in the job application package. A job description will list these items under the "How to Apply" section, and they are the things the hiring manager will want to see before considering an applicant for a position. Credentials include diplomas, certifications, discharge papers, licenses, and registrations. Credentials are required with the submission of the application package because they reflect basic requirements of the position. If an applicant lacks any of the requested credentials, then he or she is not qualified for the position and will not be considered. If a requested credential is omitted from the application package, the applicant will not be considered even if he or she does in fact have the credential. For example, if a job description asks you to send a copy of your college diploma and you forget or cannot find it, the hiring manager will discard your application.

Minimum standards to be considered for a position

Each job description will provide the pay grade for the job. This will provide you with some basic information regarding the level of experience and education the hiring manager is looking for. *See Appendix F for a complete list of pay grades.* It is important to keep in mind that the federal government, unlike many private sector employers, will take into consideration work experience in place of education level. According to the USAJOBS website, jobs listed as GS-2 pay grade coordinate with a high school education level. Jobs listed as GS-7 are at a bachelor's degree level, jobs listed as GS-9 are at a master's degree level, and jobs listed as GS-11 are at a Ph.D. education level. The GS level for a position denotes the educational level expected even when it is not stated outright. For example, if a job description indicates an applicant should have a minimum of a bachelor's degree, but it is a GS-8 or GS-9 position, the hiring manager is more likely to look for someone with a master's degree even though a bachelor's degree is acceptable. But, an applicant with a bachelor's degree and also several years of professional experience in the position being filled would be considered. Obviously, if the job is for a position requiring a license, such as a doctor, psychiatrist, or dentist, the proper licenses will need to be current and verifiable.

Reading the fine print on who can apply

Any number of factors can affect who is chosen to fill a particular position. The "fine print" is all located in the job description. Once again, it is very important to read the entire job description carefully. Each job posting will be broken up into sections, some of which have already been discussed in this book. The following lists the sections an applicant will find in a job posting and a description of the information located in that section:

- **Job title:** The job title will give the name of the position.

- **Department:** The department section will provide the name of hiring department.

- **Agency:** The agency section will list the name of the hiring agency, which is the agency the above listed department is a part of.

- **Job announcement number:** Knowing the job announcement number will allow you to quickly search for the job description again. You will also need it when you write your résumé. All federal résumés must include the job reference number at the top.

- **Salary range:** The salary range tells you the range of possible starting pay for the position.

- **Series and grade:** Every position is assigned a series number. If you are looking for a specific position regardless of the agency or department, you can look up the position's series number on the USAJOBS website. For example, Community Planning Series is GS-020, Social Work Series is GS-185, and the Forestry Technician Series is GS-462. If you find the series number for the position you want to apply for, you can use it to perform an advanced search. When you start your job search, you can opt for an advanced search. You can type in the series number for the position you are looking for, and you will be provided with only jobs that match the series number. Likewise, every job has an assigned salary grade, and an applicant can search for a job based on the salary grade.

- **Open period:** This is the specific time that application packets will be accepted.

- **Position information:** The position information will show whether the position is full- or part-time and temporary or permanent.

- **Duty location:** This section will provide the physical location of the job.

- **Who might be considered:** This section will provide the most basic qualification, such as U.S. citizen or nurse practitioner.

- **Job summary:** This section will provide a brief summary of the position and/or agency the position is within. It might include the mission of the agency and how the position fits within the overall mission. This section of the posting is generally written to attract applicants.

- **Key requirements:** This section will cover a short list of basic requirements for the job. It will be a bulleted list, and the requirements on this list are non-negotiable.

- **Major duties:** This section will highlight all the main responsibilities expected of the person filling the position. An applicant's ability to successfully complete the major duties will determine his or her chances of being hired into the position. This section might also include special instructions that should be taken into consideration. For example, one job taken from the USAJOBS website listed the following under major duties: "Spouses of active duty military members might be eligible for consideration under DEU competitive examining." This means that for this particular position, preference will be given to the spouses of active military personnel. Depending on the applicant, this information might affect his or her decision to apply for the position depending on whether that information will work to his or her advantage or disadvantage.

- **Qualifications:** The qualifications are, once again, a comprehensive list of the credentials, skills, and qualities the hiring manager is looking for in an applicant. This is the section to start in if an applicant wants to know whether he or she is qualified for a position.

- **How you will be evaluated:** This section covers what the hiring manager will be looking at when making a hiring decision.

- **Benefits:** Many job posts will also have a section titled "Benefits." This section will summarize the federal government employee benefits, which can also be found on the OPM website (**www.opm. gov**). However, it is important to read this section because it might list some benefits that are specific to that agency.

- **Other information:** This section will cover anything else an applicant will need to know but did not fit into the other sections. This section can also be used to reiterate information that is very important for the applicant to understand. The following are two examples of information in the "Other Information" section that were found in job ads listed on the USAJOBS website.

  o **Example 1:** You will be required to serve a probationary period of two years.

  o **Example 2:** Males born after December 31, 1959, must be registered or exempt from Selective Service.

- **How to apply:** This section provides the applicant with the step-by-step instructions on how to apply for the position. It is very important that applicants who want to be considered follow these instructions exactly. This section will also provide the date and time deadline for applications. Late applications are not accepted or considered.

- **Additional documents to be forwarded to or required documents:** This section will provide a list of all the credentials and documents the hiring manager will need along with the application package. This section will instruct you on exactly how the documents should be delivered to the hiring manager and how they should be labeled.

- **Contact information:** This section will provide the contact information for the department receiving the application packages. Many job postings will also provide the name of a contact person in case an applicant has any questions.

- **What to expect next:** This section will provide information about the immediate next step. This section will be brief and will not cover the entire process for filling the position, but it will tell the applicant what to expect. The following are two examples of the details often provided in this section found in job postings listed on the USAJOBS website.

  o **Example 1:** Once the human resources staff receives your complete application, you will be notified of your rating and/or referral to the hiring official.

  o **Example 2:** Once your completed application is received, we will conduct an evaluation of your qualifications. The most highly qualified candidates will be referred to the hiring manager for further consideration and possible interview.

At the end of the job posting, applicants are provided with links to the EEO policy statement, reasonable accommodation policy statement, veterans' information, and legal and regulatory guidance.

HOW THE FEDERAL GOVERNMENT HIRING SYSTEM HAS CHANGED

The federal government used to advertise job openings in a variety of ways, including paid ads and job fairs. Each department promoted their own positions, and the system as a whole was unreliable. Federal job openings were often hard to find. During this time, searching for a position was easier to do by agency instead of by position, which limited applicants' options in employment opportunities. Applications were available from each hiring department and varied from department to department. Requesting an application also took more time, as they were sent out through the mail. Because each department handled its own job openings, there was little consistency in the hiring process. There was also no consistency in the length of time it took an agency to process applications. All correspondence was done through the U.S. Postal Service, which added to the amount of time the hiring process took.

From paper to high technology

Before the federal government moved to online applications and allowing applicants to build their résumés online, it used the traditional application methods. An applicant would get an application through the specific agency or department hiring, from a job fair, or for college students, through their university. The applicant would fill out the application by hand or on a typewriter, and then mail it back along with his or her résumé, cover letter, and any credentials listed in the job application. The applicant would then have to wait until the application was received and reviewed. If the applicant was still in the running for the position, he or she would be sent forms to fill out, which would provide the federal government with all his or her information regarding past employment, education, and reference checks. The applicant would fill out an extensive questionnaire on a fill-in-the-bubble sheet. After the forms were filled out, they would need to be mailed back, and again, the applicant would wait for a response. After receiving the forms back, the hiring department would have to go through the entire packet and verify all the information, which included running criminal and background checks. This process took an inordinately long time.

CASE STUDY: ADVICE FOR RECENT COLLEGE GRADUATES

Erik Waggoner
Contract specialist
Bureau of Prisons

I applied to the federal government before everything was done online. I had to create my own résumé; although, I would have liked to be able to use the résumé builder at the time. I use it now to keep my résumé updated. Since joining the Bureau of Prisons, I have been promoted several times, which included three out-of-state moves. I needed an updated résumé each time I applied for a new position.

I would recommend that perspective employees who are fresh out of college talk up their experience as much as possible. Obviously, they should be completely honest, but they should take the time to really think about everything they did or learned while in each position. They can also add large class projects they participated in if the project could somehow be applied to the position for which they are applying.

I think the recent changes in the hiring process, which mainly eliminated KSAs (knowledge, skills, abilities), will really help applicants with little work experience. Sometimes, when applicants do not have a lot of work experience, they find it hard to write about examples that demonstrate certain skills. However, they might be very qualified for the open position. Eliminating the KSAs allows the hiring staff and managers to base their decision primarily on the résumé.

Since the introduction of the online job boards and online applications, there is no need for paper forms of any kind for most departments and positions. The applications are available online. The résumé and cover letter can be created and submitted online. Any required questionnaires can be downloaded, completed, and submitted online. The applicant will be notified through e-mail when the application was received. Even the extensive criminal and background checks are completed online by the hiring department. The entire hiring process has been sped up considerably by converting to an online process.

What you need to know about the résumé builder

The résumé builder is a program that will enable you to create your résumé online. The résumé builder provides boxes to fill in the answers for each section, as well as a spell check and word count feature. Each section of a federal résumé and cover letter has a maximum word count to prevent applicants from supplying too much unnecessary information. For that reason, it is important to be aware of word choice when writing. You want your résumé and cover letter to be detailed and descriptive while using active language and short, concise sentences.

The résumé builder will also allow you to save résumés that are not complete. This allows you to go back and edit the résumé later and to update it as you gain experience or education. Each profile can save up to five résumés. This allows users to create multiple résumés tailored to different positions for which they might be applying. Updating or editing the résumé is simple. You simply sign into your account, open your saved résumé, and click "Edit." When you are finished with the résumé, you upload it into an application when applying for a job through the USAJOBS website.

Creating your online profile and résumé before you apply

Your online profile will be located on the USAJOBS website. Your profile page will allow you to save job search results and up to five résumés. You can also track the jobs you have already applied for through your online profile. Creating an online profile with the USAJOBS website only takes a minute and requires an active e-mail address. Once you create your online profile, use the résumé builder to create your résumé. Through your online profile, you also have the power to make your résumé searchable once it is finished and ready to be seen.

Both an online profile and résumé must be created before you will be able to apply for a position through the USAJOBS website. The best thing to do is to create the profile first, and then search the job database for the position or positions you want to apply for. After you have found a position to apply for, you can save the search results and then go back to creating the résumé. After the résumé is finished, you can apply for the position. Conveniently, when you save a search to your profile, the USAJOBS website will automatically send you an e-mail notification when a new job fitting your search parameters is posted.

Presidential Memorandum
Improving the Federal Recruitment and Hiring Process
May 11, 2010

Although there have been references made to the recent changes made in the Federal hiring process, it is important to understand the overall impact of these changes. This memorandum puts into effect the largest changes to the Federal hiring process since the job descriptions and application process went online. Here is an overview of the changes going into effect.

- Elimination of essay style questions, also known as KSAs. KSA stood for Knowledge, Skills, and Ability. Eliminating the KSA provides less work for candidates during the initial application process, but it also eliminates a means for them to promote themselves. Without the KSAs, hiring managers can only rely on the cover letter and résumé for key words and phrases. One clear benefit of eliminating the KSAs is moving the focus away from the candidates writing style and focusing it squarely on the content of their cover letter and résumé.

- Agencies will also move away from the "rule of 3" approach to hiring and adopt a "category rating" method. Under the "rule of 3" approach, all applications were given a score based on a number of factors, including key word usage and KSAs. Once all the applications were scored the hiring managers would select a candidate only from the top three scoring applicants. The "category rating" approach allows hiring managers to take different things into account and interview applicants who may not have scored high initially.

- Hiring managers and supervisors are expected to participate more in the overall hiring process beyond making the final selection. Hiring managers and supervisors will also be held accountable for the hiring selections being made.

- Each agency will be responsible for reducing the amount of time it takes to fill mission-critical positions. They will also need to analyze issues within their hiring process, and create a plan to deal with those issues.

- Every agency hiring manager will be provided with specialized training on ways to efficiently recruit new employees in a timely manner.

- The role of the USAJOBS website will be expanding to include notification for candidates on their application status throughout the hiring process. There will also be research done to see how the capacity of the USAJOBS website can be increased.

- OPM will develop a plan for each agency to promote diversity in the Federal workforce. This includes hiring more veterans and individuals with disabilities.

- OPM has also been put in charge of improving the content and quality of job announcements, evaluating the Federal Career Intern Program, and evaluating the effectiveness of shared registers, which are used to fill positions that are common in multiple agencies.

Each of these changes will be initiated, if not completed by November 1, 2010. Compliance with this memorandum is not voluntary, and OPM will be conducting annual reviews to study the effectiveness of the changes being made.

GETTING TO KNOW YOUR WAY AROUND THE U.S. OFFICE OF PERSONNEL MANAGEMENT (OPM)

Anyone looking to be hired, and even those already employed by the federal government, will want to be familiar with the U.S. Office of Personnel Management (OPM) website (**www.opm.gov**). The OPM is the human resources department for the entire federal government. When considering a job with the federal government, exploring this website should be your first step.

For prospective employees, the OPM website gives detailed information regarding employee benefits, including medical, vacation, retirement, and types of insurance offered. It also provides current news and information affecting federal employees. There are also links to the job boards including USAJOBS.com and the official Recovery website (**www.recovery.gov**), which details information regarding the Recovery Act. The OPM website also presents an overview of the different types of positions available, including internships and part-time employment.

For current employees, the OPM website provides information on the multiple health insurance plans offered by the federal government, detailed retirement information, links to different documents and websites covering their rights as federal employees, help for veterans and disabled employees, and information on how to file an official complaint. It also offers statistical information on federal employment and current news events that might affect federal employees.

For any questions related to federal government pay, benefits, or specific questions related to health, life, or long-term disability insurance, you should check the OPM website before trying to contact someone in person. This website can answer most questions. It also supplies a variety of different forms related to insurance, pay, and benefits, which can be downloaded easily. Centralizing human resources needs into one office for the entire federal government eliminates possible misunderstandings or misinterpretation, as OPM applies to all federal employees regardless of agency or department.

DIFFERENT RULES YOU NEED TO KNOW BEFORE APPLYING TO THE FEDERAL GOVERNMENT

When you get a job working for the federal government, you are serving the taxpayers, and any mistakes you make can become public very quickly. Federal jobs also require every applicant to take a drug test. Hiring managers also are allowed to ask applicants about possible drug use. An applicant can be denied employment if they refuse background or security checks. Although these elements might be present in some private sector positions, they are present and consistent in all federal employment screenings at all levels of employment. The federal government can also require an applicant to undergo physical or psychological tests to determine his or her ability to fulfill major duties of the position.

Your mistakes could become public

When you create an online profile on the USAJOBS website, you can choose to have your résumé searchable or not searchable. When a résumé is marked as searchable, anyone with access to the website will have access to the résumé. This means managers or job recruiters could view it. Although you can make changes to your résumé after you have created your online profile, you cannot change what other people have already read. Applicants also cannot stop others from saving the résumé, printing it, or posting it somewhere else. However, the fact that many people can review it should not sway an applicant from making his or her résumé searchable. Federal recruiters can look at résumés posted on the USAJOBS website. You might be offered a position if you have a specific skill a recruiter is looking for.

Making a résumé unsearchable means that it will only be seen by the people an applicant sends the résumé to. It is more common for people to do this once they are already employed by the federal government and not looking to move. For prospective employees, however, making a résumé searchable might open them up to an opportunity they did not even know existed. An applicant should keep his or her résumé unsearchable until it is completed and if an applicant registers for an open and continuous position.

Embellishing on your résumé might cost you the job

Everything written in the résumé and cover letter is verified, which includes education, past work experience, certifications, and military status. If a hiring manager finds that an applicant embellished on his or her résumé, the application packet will be discarded from the pool of applicants. If the lie is not discovered until after the employee is hired, that person's job will be at risk, and he or she might not be considered for future federal positions.

Another situation in which embellishing on a résumé can seriously hurt the applicant is in contract positions. *Contract positions will be covered extensively in Chapter 9.* Contracted employees sign a contract with the federal agency for which they are working. Embellishing on a résumé for a contract position can result in the contract being canceled, and the applicant could lose out on future opportunities with federal government contracts.

Although not treated as a crime, embellishing on a résumé can carry significant consequences. In 2004, Laura Callahan, senior director of the Homeland Security Department's Chief Information Officer's department, resigned after it was discovered that her diplomas came from a diploma mill and not a real university. Although she made it through the background check conducted when she was hired into the federal government, her fake degrees were discovered while she was being investigated for top-secret security clearance. Callahan resigned after her deception was discovered.

You might be under the microscope

Once you submit your application and give the hiring manager permission to complete the mandatory background checks, you cannot stop them from looking at or seeing certain things. If you have outstanding warrants, liens, or child support payments, these will all be uncovered and action can be taken against you in these matters. The federal government will go back seven years into your history. Hiring personnel will review your employment history, criminal background, and credit checks. They will look into all the places you claim to have lived, and they will contact your previous employers as well as neighbors or family members. They will have you sit through an "integrity interview." During this interview, they will ask you questions regarding questionable or illegal activities that might not be in an official record, such as personal drug use.

WHAT IS IMPORTANT TO A FEDERAL GOVERNMENT HIRING MANAGER?

Hiring managers do not want to spend the time micromanaging or training new employees on the basic functions of the job. Ideally, a federal hiring manager wants to hire someone who will hit the ground running. Hiring managers determine an applicant's ability to fill the position with minimal direct supervision by looking at his or her experience. If an applicant has a great deal of experience in a field closely related to the position being filled, it is likely that the applicant will be invited in for an interview.

The best way for an applicant to demonstrate his or her ability to fill a position and exceed the expectations of the hiring manager is to demonstrate how much he or she wants to be hired. Taking time to craft the perfect résumé and cover letter and follow application instructions exactly will help an applicant demonstrate his or her strong desire for the position. The application will also ask for a great deal of personal and contact information. Besides the résumé and cover letter, the application is not something that can be filled out quickly or with little thought.

CHAPTER 3

The Federal Application Process

Bakers know that making bread from scratch is a process. You cannot just throw all the ingredients in a baking dish and hope for the best. The ingredients need to be added together in a specific order, the water needs to be a specific temperature, and the dough needs time to rise. The baker must take the time to knead and form the dough before placing it in the oven. The oven needs to be heated to a specific temperature, and the dough needs to be in the oven for a specific amount of time. If the baker takes the time to follow the steps closely, the result will be golden-brown, deliciously fresh bread.

Applying for a federal job is much like baking bread. It is not hard, and if you follow the steps laid out for you and take your time, the result can be a satisfying job with the federal government. If you upload a generically made résumé that you have already used for three other jobs, a cover letter and questionnaire that were not proofread, and fail to follow the directions, you will be settling for a job somewhere else. The mass mailing technique will not work. Applying for a federal job is a process that you cannot rush through and still expect positive results.

APPLYING FOR A FEDERAL JOB: THE PROCESS

An applicant will go through several steps when applying for a federal position, and these steps make up a very lengthy and detailed process. It is important to understand the process, so even after you are finished with your part, you have an idea of what is happening with your application packet. The following is a list of steps in the process of applying for a federal job:

1. Find a job on one of the job boards. The largest online job board is on the USAJOBS website. *There are also other online job boards, which will be explained in detail in Chapter 4.* You can search for jobs by position, agency, department, pay grade, or location. Applicants can also chose to search by position series number if they know exactly what position they are looking for.

2. Carefully read the job description for the position you are interested in to be sure you are fully qualified and understand the directions for applying to the position. Save the job description in your online profile and/or print the job description, so you can refer back to it as you prepare your résumé and cover letter.

3. Based on the information supplied in the job description, create your résumé and cover letter. Make sure they are focused and well organized. *The process of crafting the perfect résumé and cover letter will be covered extensively in Chapters 7 and 8.*

4. Fill out the application, questionnaire, and any other requirements listed in the job description. The requirements for the application will vary from one position to the next. It is important to include everything asked of you in the job description.

5. Organize all your credentials, follow the instructions for applying, and submit your application packet. Sometimes you will be instructed to submit the application, résumé, and cover letter online and then be given an address or fax number to send copies of your credentials to.

6. When your application is received, you will receive a confirmation e-mail.

7. Once your application packet is submitted, it will go through the agency database and to the human resources staff. The human resources staff will review the application to determine if you are eligible for the position. The staff will also read your résumé and cover letter to score them based on a predetermined scoring system to determine the level of qualification. This step is sometimes completed by an automated system that processes the forms looking for keyword usage.

8. After the applications, résumés, and cover letters are evaluated, the applicants are divided into either rejected or accepted categories.

9. The accepted applications are sent to the hiring manager. The hiring manager can than choose to access the applicants further through interviews and follow-up questionnaires or decide against all the candidates. The applications forwarded to the hiring manager are for the people determined qualified by the human resource staff, but the hiring manager is not required to choose from those applications. The manager also is not required to interview multiple candidates.

REGISTERING FOR JOBS

Some positions in the federal government are categorized as "open and continuous." These are positions that are always in need. For example, correctional officers are always needed because of the constantly growing and expanding needs of the correctional system. Instead of listing job postings for every facility looking to fill the position, there are basic job descriptions available that apply to the position regardless of the facility. For these positions, applicants can register for the position. Applicants submit their application, résumé, cover letter, and credentials, and indicate the top three facilities at which they would want to work. They are not contacted until a position becomes available at a facility listed in their top three choices, and their information is forwarded to that facility's human resources staff for evaluation.

Federal prisons are always in need of correctional officers, so the position remains open and continuous. Once an applicant registers for a position, their information will remain on file for one year. If in that year a position did not become available at the applicant's requested facility, he or she must re-register. When the applicant re-registers, he or she can choose to list new preference facilities or can keep the original three and continue waiting for an open position.

Almost all federal jobs are posted on the USAJOBS website. Even if the hiring agency is using a different website for its online application process, the job will be posted to the USAJOBS website, and a link to the other website is provided in the job description. When an applicant wants to register for an open and continuous position, he or she will do so on the USAJOBS website. In order to register for a position, an applicant must set up an online profile and either create or upload a résumé to his or her USAJOBS' profile. Once the applicant has done that, he or she will be registered for any position. Open and continuous positions used to be handled through the position's agency, but now they are handled through the USAJOBS website — just like the location-specific job openings that have deadlines.

PLAN ON SPENDING TIME ON A LENGTHY PROCESS

Every aspect of applying for a federal job has the potential to be time-consuming and lengthy. Be prepared to spend plenty of time preparing your résumé to make sure it reflects the highest level of quality. Once your résumé is submitted, it might take weeks or even months before you will hear back from the hiring department. Even after you are called in for an interview, it could take several more weeks for the hiring manager to make a decision. Do not wait to hear back from one specific position before applying for another position. It is acceptable to apply for several positions simultaneously.

CASE STUDY: USING ENTRY-LEVEL POSITIONS TO GET AHEAD

Cathy Mathis
Correctional treatment specialist
Federal Bureau of Prisons

When I first started with the Bureau nearly 20 years ago, the application process was long and done through the mail. Now, everything is done online, which I find much easier. I have used the USAJOBS résumé builder numerous times when applying for promotions and other positions. I definitely recommend the résumé builder to others. Being able to save multiple copies of your résumé and update it at anytime has been extremely helpful and has saved me a great deal of time. For a candidate new to USAJOBS, I would recommend playing around with the résumé builder a little. Create a résumé and then print it out, so you can see how it will be formatted. Although it is different, I much prefer it over having to create a résumé on my own.

Individuals who are hoping to get a position in the federal government but do not have specific training, such as lawyers or medical personnel, should try for entry-level positions. These positions include clerical ones or correctional officers in the Bureau of Prisons. Although the position might not be what they were hoping for, it will be a lot easier for them to get a different position once they are already inside. I think the biggest mistake people make when trying to get a federal position is not being specific enough about their experience. Candidates will come into interviews discussing the philosophies they learned in their criminal justice classes, but they fail to mention whether or not they have direct supervisory experience. Candidates need to be very specific in what experience they have and how it can be applied to the position being hired. Candidates also need to keep in mind that work experience is not the only thing looked at. Quasi-professional experience, volunteer work, and internships all count as applicable experienced.

Overall, the hiring process is still a bit lengthy. Candidates for entry-level positions have to undergo an integrity interview. This interview will cover personal background information including questions regarding their financial condition, possible criminal record, or drug use. It is very important to be honest during this interview, even if you do not think it is the answer the interviewer wants to hear.

The integrity interview will be with a human resources staff member. The second interview will be a panel interview. This will be with generally three or four people, and it will be what most people consider a typical job interview. The questions will all revolve around the candidates experience and ability to handle the job. The candidate will then be asked a few scenario questions. Working in a federal prison is a unique situation, and hiring managers want to make sure you can handle yourself in situations that might arise. For example, an interviewer might ask the candidate what he or she would do if two inmates start fighting and one pulls out a weapon. Obviously, we have policies in place, which the candidate is not aware of. The purpose the question is to see if they would use common sense and react ethically.

RÉSUMÉS AND COVER LETTERS: A SMALL PART OF THE FEDERAL GOVERNMENT'S EXTENSIVE HIRING PROCESS

It has been established that the federal hiring process is laborious. Although the résumé and cover letter are crucial elements of the application package, they are not the only elements. The application is also scrutinized during the application process, and the background checks can make or break an individual's opportunity to work for the federal government. An applicant can be given a probationary or conditional position in a variety of scenarios In this situation, an applicant will be hired pending the completion of a period of time or specific test. For example, some positions might require a psychological exam or a bona fide occupational qualification (BFOQ), which is an ability or attribute that an employer will consider when prior to hiring an applicant. In that case, a new employee's employment might be terminated if he or she does not fulfill or pass the conditional requirements.

Another important element of the hiring process is the interview. *Interviews will be discussed in more detail in Chapter 4.* After the human resources staff qualifies applicants, and their information has been forwarded to the hiring manager, they might be called in for an interview. They were offered an interview based on the quality of their résumé in demonstrating their fulfillment of the position qualifications. The interview is the applicant's opportunity to solidify the hiring manger's decision. An applicant should be as prepared and professional for the interview as they were preparing their résumé.

SIMILARITIES AND DIFFERENCES BETWEEN THE APPLICATION PROCESSES: FEDERAL JOBS VERSUS PRIVATE SECTOR JOBS

Often, it is easiest to examine something when comparing it to something we already understand. Most people understand and can recognize the basic elements of a private sector résumé. Comparing a federal résumé to a private sector résumé allows people to see the clear differences between the two. A private sector résumé is not suitable when applying for a federal position. Likewise, a federal résumé would be considered too long and detailed for a private sector job.

Similarities

Although the differences between a résumé for a federal job and one for a private sector job are more readily available to discuss, there are some similarities between the two. There is the most basic information an employer needs and wants to know about an applicant regardless of who the employer is or what the open position is. Understanding what the employer is looking for is the most important aspect of applying for a job.

Contact and other information will be the same

Applicants will supply all the same contact information for a federal job as they would a private sector job. It is perfectly acceptable to supply e-mail addresses and cell phone numbers for contact information. Because most applications are completed online and confirmations are sent through e-mail, it is also acceptable to follow-up through e-mail to the person listed under the contact information in the job description. Although the federal applications will ask for more information, it will be the same type of information private sector applications require. For example, on a private sector résumé, applicants might list the position they are applying for under the objectives section. On a federal résumé, applicants are required to list the position and job description number at the top of the résumé.

Job experience and accomplishments do count

Past job experience and accomplishments are just as important to federal hiring managers as they are to private sector managers. Federal hiring managers will take past experiences and accomplishments into consideration when determining whether an applicant can fulfill all the major duties of the position. The federal government is more diligent in verifying past employment and contacting former supervisors and co-workers. The private sector looks at job experience directly related to the open position. The federal government will look at experience that was loosely related or that fulfilled portions of the major duties. Honesty is also very important when describing job experience and accomplishments. If upon verification it is discovered that an applicant was not completely honest, his or her application will be discarded. Applicants will also need to account for any gaps in their work history.

Differences

Although there are clearly several similarities between a résumé and cover letter for a federal position and one for a private sector position, applicants should be aware of a few important differences. Being aware of the differences will allow applicants the opportunity to create the best possible résumé given their specific skills, education, and experience. The goal in writing a résumé and cover letter is to impress the hiring staff and manager enough to want to meet you in person.

Sometimes more is better

Because the goals of private sector employers are driven by profits, the information they are most interested in is how an applicant's past experience and education can be used to the advantage of their company. The federal government is looking for more than that. Federal hiring managers are looking for individuals who can be a part of a cohesive team that works together toward a common goal. Federal employees should be hard working, conscientious, and professional at all times.

In the private sector, being overqualified for a position is often a negative, and applications will be discarded if the applicant is deemed overqualified. The federal government, however, does not penalize people for being highly qualified because eagerness and willing to grow and promote within the agency are strongly desired traits. The federal government wants employees with an abundance of related experience so they can take on their new position with minimal supervision.

History is important

History is important to a federal hiring manager because it is the best indicator of future activity and progress. Hiring managers will look at your past work history and experiences. They will also look at past job performance and willingness to go the extra mile for the employer. Job history is very important in determining if the applicant is qualified, as well as deciding if the applicant is the right fit for the position and the department. Work history is not the only aspect hiring managers will look at, however.

Hiring managers require educational and work credentials in order to get a full picture of your training leading up to the present time. The background checks conducted are also a testament to your past. Bad credit can prevent an applicant from being hired for a position if the hiring manager feels the employee will be in a position to be tempted by bribery or blackmail. Criminal histories are looked at on a case-by-case basis because past criminal activity is not always an indicator of future problems.

Résumés and cover letters are a part of the federal application process

Private sector employers rely completely on an applicant's résumé and cover letter to make a decision on whether to invite an applicant for an interview.

They then take the information they gain from the interview and make a decision on whether to hire the applicant. Some private sector employers might run a background check, but that varies greatly.

The federal government, on the other hand, looks at the applicant's application, résumé, cover letter, exam results (if an exam was required), and credentials to decide whether the applicant will be invited in for an interview. The government will then take all the information it already has and add the interview responses, credit check, and criminal check to make a final decision. The hiring process in the federal government is much more in-depth than the private sector, considering far more elements for employment.

It is not as simple as going to a job website and clicking "Apply"

Although many federal jobs can be applied for online, the application process is still much lengthier than simply posting a résumé online like you can with many popular employment search websites. You must prepare your résumé and cover letter prior to applying and gather and provide credentials according to the instructions provided in the job description. It is a good idea to have others review your résumé and cover letter prior to submitting it. This exercise can provide you with useful feedback regarding presentation and organization of the information and ensure that you included all materials and items.

The single-page rule does not apply

In the private sector, it is strongly encouraged that a résumé be no longer than one page. Longer résumés tend to have too much unnecessary information, descriptive language, or go back too far in work history. The federal government, however, wants as much information as an applicant is able to provide. Although you should still avoid useless information or descriptions, you should provide your entire career-related work history. You should provide all of your accomplishments, certifications, special training, education, computer skills, and other involvements. You can also briefly provide information regarding volunteer positions or significant hobbies.

This information is considered relevant because it speaks to the type of person the applicant is. Federal résumés are expected to be longer than one page; however, it is important to remember that hiring managers are very busy people, and they do not want to be tied up reading irrelevant information in an applicant's résumé.

You can apply to multiple federal government positions without being tagged a chronic job applicant

Although you want to be sure you only apply for jobs that you are qualified for, you can apply for multiple jobs simultaneously. You can apply for the same or similar positions in multiple agencies, or you can apply for multiple positions within one agency. At any point in the job application process, you can withdraw yourself from consideration. If you have applied for multiple jobs, and you are offered a job, you can withdraw your application for the other positions. If you apply for several positions and are turned down for all of them, you should review your résumé and cover letter. It is possible that you are being eliminated due to a poorly crafted résumé. It is also possible you are applying for jobs for which you are not qualified.

Unlike in private industry, different departments and divisions usually mean different hiring managers

Each hiring department will have its own hiring manager and staff, so hiring managers will not necessarily know how many other positions you have applied for. You will not risk being hired into another position if you interview with one hiring manager and the interview does not go well. This is clearly different than the private sector. Typically, a private-sector company will have one hiring or human resource department that will review all the applications and handle all the interviews for the entire company. Experiencing the hiring process from multiple agencies or departments will enable you to better understand the actual application of the hiring process.

Why the application process is so different

Employees of the federal government are working for the taxpayers. They have a specific goal that in some way serves the country, and they have a responsibility to the taxpayers to accomplish that goal. The majority of federal employees understand the goal and importance of their agency. This knowledge gives federal employees a sense of pride in their work and a drive toward completing their job to their highest ability. Hiring managers within the federal government have to take into consideration the needs of the department and the position when hiring someone. This is, in part, why the application process for a federal job is so different than the application process for a private sector job. The heads of federal agencies have to answer to the taxpayers, so they want to ensure they have the most highly qualified people working in their agency.

On the other hand, private-sector jobs are driven by profits. Every employee's goal is to help maximize the profits of the company. The shareholders, who make money when the company is profitable, expect the employees to work toward maximizing the profits. This knowledge sometimes leads to employees feeling indifferent or even resentful toward their employer. Federal positions provide employees with a sense of altruism, which is not present when the overall goal of the position is to make money for the sake of making money.

SECURITY ISSUES

When applying for a federal job, there are some security issues to be aware of as far as information is concerned. Positions that require high security clearance are those in which the employees will have access to important materials, files, and information. Security is important for all federal positions, which is why credit and criminal checks are standard. However, some federal jobs require a high degree of security because of the nature of the position. Jobs in the Central Intelligence Agency, National Security Agency, Defense Intelligence Agency, and National Imagery and Mapping Agency do not include their employee numbers in the national statistics due to security issues. These departments deal directly with the security of the nation, and the employee screening process is extremely rigorous. This screening process makes it more difficult to obtain a position in highly secure departments.

Knowing who is hired is very important

The constant fear of a terrorist attack makes it very important to know who is being hired for federal positions. This is particularly true for individuals being hired into positions involving access to classified information. This is why security clearances are ranked by importance. The higher the security clearance an employee is given, the more intense the background investigation will be. Under the new changes being made to the hiring system, hiring managers are taking personal responsibility for the people being hired into their departments. This increases their motivation to complete a thorough investigation into the candidate's past. Knowing who is being hired is also vitally important to make sure every federal employee is trained and capable of successfully completed the task they are assigned.

Background checks

Background checks will include a credit check. Applicants with bad credit or a high amount of debt will be barred from many positions. If an applicant has financial problems, the federal government will not take the risk of putting him or her in a high security or confidential position where they could be bribed or blackmailed for information or other resources. For positions in accounting or finance, bad credit can also cause a hiring manager to call into question the applicant's ability to handle money and keep accurate records.

The federal government will also perform a National Crime Information Center (NCIC) check on all prospective applicants. The NCIC is maintained by the FBI and contains a record of all criminal activity, stolen property, and missing persons. The information is gathered from the FBI, federal law enforcement, state law enforcement, local police, foreign criminal justice agencies, and authorized courts. An applicant's entire FBI file will be made available to the hiring manager for review. Information in these reports can include everything from murder to speeding tickets. For high-security positions, the hiring manager will also look into the applicant's social affiliations for any indications of ulterior motives. Social affiliations might include religious groups, social groups, or political organizations.

The USA PATRIOT Act

The title USA PATRIOT Act is an acronym that stands for Uniting and Strengthening America by Providing Appropriate Tools Required to Intercept and Obstruct Terrorism Act of 2001. This Act was put into effect following the terrorist attacks of September 11, 2001. The USA PATRIOT Act was enacted by a bipartisan vote of Congress. The goal of the USA PATRIOT Act is to eliminate the threat of terrorism. Elements of this act include allowing law enforcement agencies to use electronic surveillance, conduct investigations without informing the person being investigated, and gain access to business records.

The USA PATRIOT Act applies to federal workforce candidates because these methods of investigation may be used to ensure no one applying for a federal position is in any way tied to a terrorist organization. The fear of terrorist connections also leads background investigations to look at political, religious, and social affiliations. The sole purpose of this act is to actively prevent another terrorist attack on U.S. soil.

Prepare for in-depth scrutiny

The federal government currently goes back seven years when conducting security checks for most positions. There are certain positions, such as those with high security clearance, that are even more in-depth and go back even further than seven years. For example, individuals hired on as Secret Service special agents go through the highest levels of security checks before they are permitted to guard the president or other high ranking officials. Applicants will be asked to supply a list of personal references, as well as work-related references. The references will be contacted and asked questions about the applicant. The questions will be designed primarily to confirm the information already provided by the applicant and gather additional information regarding the applicant's abilities and experience. The hiring manager might also send letters to random neighbors, friends, and family requesting information about the applicant. Part of the goal in this process is to verify the honesty of the applicant's responses in the questionnaire and during the integrity interview.

Applicants can prepare for this in-depth scrutiny by telling friends and family someone from the agency you are applying to may contact them. The applicant can also contact his or her previous employers to let them know that someone within the agency may be contacting them. This will prevent the people from being surprised, thrown off, or even angered by the interaction.

An applicant can also work to clear up his or her credit prior to applying for a federal position. Often, individuals have bad marks on their credit report that are outdated or could be removed from their credit report. To do this, they should obtain copies of each of the three reports: Equifax, TransUnion, and Experian. It is important to obtain reports from all three credit agencies because different companies report to different agencies. It is possible to have negative marks on one credit report that are not on the other credit reports. Review each credit report carefully and highlight any negative marks that could be removed. Contact the creditor involved to request they contact the credit agency. If that does not work, applicants should file a dispute with the credit agency. The applicant should also be sure to pay all his or her bills on time and pay off any miscellaneous debts if possible.

To prepare for a background check or investigations, candidates can also search for themselves through an Internet search engine, such as Google™. You might be surprised about what turns up, such as news articles, photos, or references made about involvement in different activities. Candidates seeking federal employment also need to be aware of what they put on social networking websites like Facebook or MySpace. This includes what you say about yourself, your friends, or your current position. It is becoming more popular for potential employers to look up Facebook or MySpace pages to ensure the integrity of the person they are dealing with. Although many argue that what is posted on a personal page should not affect their employment possibilities, it certainly can. Candidates should also avoid having questionable photos of themselves posted in the Internet. Agencies are not likely to hire individuals who might be involved in a scandal revolving around information or photos found on a social networking website.

Security clearances

An applicant can receive a security clearance after he or she is hired into the federal government. Employees who handle or have access to classified documents or work in secured locations are eligible for security clearance. These positions are referred to as "sensitive" positions, which the federal government defines as "any position, by virtue of their nature, (that) could bring about a material adverse effect on national security." There are three categories of security clearance:

1. **Confidential:** These security clearances are the easiest to obtain and require background checks conducted by the agency sponsoring the application. For example, the FBI can run its own check to give FBI agents confidential security clearance. This security clearance is given to individuals who have access to documents that, if disclosed, could pose a reasonable threat to national security. Individuals with confidential security clearance need to be reinvestigated every 15 years.

2. **Secret:** This level of security clearance is for employees with access to information and documents and that carry the possibility of an expected threat to national security if disclosed. An employee with secret security clearance must be reinvestigated every ten years. In addition, the Defense Security Service (DSS) must conduct the investigation.

3. **Top secret:** This is the highest level of security clearance. Top-secret security clearance is for individuals with access to information that, if disclosed, could cause immediate and grave damage to national security. Employees with this level of clearance are also investigated by the DSS, but they are investigated every five years. This security clearance also requires a Single Scope Background Investigation (SSBI), which typically takes four to eight months, but it can take up to one year. An SSBI is very extensive and includes the following:

    •   National Agency Check for both the applicant and the applicant's spouse or partner

- Verification of the applicant's birth date and location to look for possible discrepancies
- Verification of the applicant's citizenship
- Verification of the applicant's educational background, which will include personal interviews with past instructors and school officials
- Verification of all the applicant's past employment for the previous seven years, which will include personal interviews with past supervisors and co-workers from each job the applicant held for more than six months
- Interviews with four references
- Interview with former spouse(s)
- Confirmation of each previous residence for the previous three years
- Verification of financial status, which will include credit checks
- Local agency checks for each residence where the applicant lived for more than six months
- Public records check to verify marriages, divorces, bankruptcies, and any court actions
- An interview with the applicant
- Subjecting the applicant to a polygraph test

In order to obtain security clearance, an employee needs to be sponsored by his or her agency. An employee cannot personally apply for security clearance. Once an employee is sponsored, he or she will need to fill out a Personnel Security Questionnaire (SF-86), be fingerprinted, and verify citizenship. That employee will then be investigated. The level of security clearance determines the type of investigation. Finally, the application goes into a phase called the adjudication phase. This is when all the information from the background checks is brought together and examined based on 13 factors predetermined by the Department of Defense.

Lots of paper work and for some jobs, polygraphs

The higher the security clearance, the more paperwork and security checks there will be. It is important to national security to ensure that dangerous or unqualified people are not put into positions that could endanger others. The applicant's paperwork will include his or her résumé, cover letter, application, and background check consent forms. At the application level, the paperwork of security clearance will not need to be completed. However, once hired, if the position requires security clearance, the new employee will be required to go through additional checks outlined in the previous section.

Applicants going into the Defense Security Service, the National Security Agency, or the Central Intelligence Agency are also required to take a polygraph. Polygraphs might be used for personnel investigations, but only with the consent of the person being investigated. Polygraphs can be used if an employee is being investigated for the unauthorized disclosure of classified information or for alleged acts of terrorism.

APPLYING FOR SPECIFIC BRANCHES OF THE FEDERAL GOVERNMENT

Some areas of federal employment do not follow the traditional application process. For example, active military has its own method of recruiting, which does not require a résumé or cover letter. Civilians in the military, legislative positions, and the positions with the U.S. Postal Service all follow a somewhat different method. If these are areas of interest for you, it is important to understand the differences before applying.

Active military duty

Active military are the men and women who serve the country as members of the armed forces. Active military does not include reservist and those in the National Guard who are not currently active. Active military includes the Army, Navy, Air Force, Marines, Coast Guard, and activated National Guard. Active military jobs are different from other positions with the federal government because they do not require a résumé or cover letter. As an all-volunteer military, service is volunteered rather than compulsory. Members are recruited, so people interesting in joining a branch of the military need to meet with a recruiter. The recruiter will explain what is involved in joining the military and what will be expected of them. Each branch of the military has its own basic training, commonly known as "boot camp." Those interested in joining active military duty will be accepted based on their ability to pass basic boot camp and, if applicable, advanced training camp. After graduating, they will be given their work orders, which will dictate their job, where they will be stationed, and for how long.

There are positions within each branch of the military that carry signing bonuses for incoming soldiers. These are high-demand positions, and signing bonuses are offered to increase possible recruitment. The soldier signs a contract promising to serve for a specific number of years in exchange for the signing bonus. If the soldier leaves the military prior to completion of the contract, he or she will be required to repay the bonus. Perspective college students can choose to join the ROTC, which will enable them to finish their schooling first and then join the active military as an officer. Each branch of the military has its own ROTC, and applying does require a résumé.

CASE STUDY: APPLYING TO THE ROTC

Zack Giddings
Air Force ROTC

The Air Force ROTC application process required several steps. First, I had to set up an online account with the Air Force ROTC scholarship application website. Then, I had to fill out the application. At some point along the way, I needed to collect a letter of reference from my Senior Aerospace Science Instructor (SASI), a copy of my high school transcript with the school's seal, my ACT/SAT scores, and some personal statements about myself and my purpose in wanting to join the United States Air Force. Then, I had to drive to the nearest Air Force ROTC unit to be interviewed.

I'm joining the AFROTC because the government will pay for tuition, books, and give me a monthly stipend. After I have gone through my years in the AFROTC with the scholarship, I am committed to the Air Force. I will be commissioned into the Air Force as a Second Lieutenant which means a higher pay, better job, and more responsibility than an Airman Basic.

I had to write a one-page résumé in a very specific format. The first section was on leadership in extracurricular activities. The second section was a list of awards and accomplishments. The third section was a list of community activities. The fourth and final section was my employment history.

I would advise students interested in the ROTC program to start early like I did or the deadline will sneak up on you quickly. Plenty of head time also makes the SASI happy.

Civilian service in the military

Civilian service positions are jobs working for one of the armed forces, but not as a member of active military. Active military personnel commit to serving in the military for a specific period, while civilian workers can leave their jobs whenever they chose to. Civilian military jobs are posted on the USAJOBS website along with other federal job openings. When searching for jobs, an applicant can search by agency, which will include the military branches. The Army and the Air Force have a large number of civilian employees, and each branch of the military has its own website dedicated to its civilian employees. Information regarding the positions and benefits offered to civilian military workers can be obtained through these websites. It is also important to note that preference is often given to the spouses of active military personnel for civilian jobs.

Applying for a civilian military job starts with finding an open position though the USAJOBS website and reading the job description carefully. An applicant can then prepare a résumé through the résumé builder or create his or her own. The applicant will then need to follow the instructions in the job description, complete the application, and provide the needed credentials. Once the applicant submits his or her application, résumé, cover letter, and credentials, the information will go to the human resource staff for the military branch posting the position. The human resource staff will determine the applicant's eligibility and qualifications and then forward the qualified applications to the hiring manager. The hiring manager will make the final decision regarding employment.

CASE STUDY: FEDERAL EMPLOYMENT: A LENGTHY PROCESS

Bob Cox
Logistics management specialist
Department of Defense

I first learned about the position through a job fair held at my former university. The idea of working for the federal government was an interest for me due to the job security a federal position offered. As a recent college graduate, I wanted to find an employer that would provide me with a stable income. I arranged the initial interview at the job fair while meeting with a recruiter. For that reason, I did not have the opportunity to use the USAJOBS résumé builder.

After the initial interview, I provided the recruiters with more information about myself through their application manager. Approximately a month following this, I participated in a teleconference with the recruiters and other potential hires, where questions and concerns were covered. From there, the hiring process transferred to the Air Force Personnel Center. Because the position was as a civilian working for the Air force, they had the final say on who was hired.

I would advise anyone seeking a position with the federal government to be patient. Despite the positive outcome of my initial interview, it took approximately four months between the time I applied for the position and when I was hired. Once you have submitted an application, do not be afraid to call or e-mail the contact person to check the status of your application. Occasionally, follow up with the agency contact person, which will keep your name fresh on their minds.

Legislative jobs and jobs in Washington, D.C.

Many legislative jobs are posted on the USAJOBS website with the other federal job openings. These jobs include administrative, maintenance, and other positions dealing with the Capitol Building, such as landscape designer. Legislative jobs might also cover the Congressional Budget Office, the General Accounting Office, and the General Printing Office. However, an applicant can check a few additional websites for specific jobs.

For example, the U.S. House of Representatives has a job board on its own website (**www.house.gov/cao-hr**). Applicants can go to this website to view job openings, submit their résumé, and view other information regarding employment. These jobs are specific to offices within the House of Representatives, such as the Office of the Law Revision Counsel and the Office of the Chief Administrative Officer. Examples of jobs offered include federal retirement specialist, financial analyst, and information systems security manager.

The U.S. Senate also has employment information on its website (**www. senate.gov/employment**). The Senate Placement Office accepts résumés and cover letters from applicants interested in working for senators. The office reviews the résumés, chooses the qualified applicants, and then refers them to senators looking for staff members. Interested applicants will also need to fill out an applicant referral form, which is available through the Senate's website.

Applicants looking for job opportunities with Congress can also use the following contacts for more information:

- **House of Representatives Job Line:** 202-226-4504
- **Senate Job Line:** 202-228-JOBS
- **Human Resources Vacancy Announcement Lists:** B227 Longworth House Office Building
- **Senate Placement Office:** Room SH-142, Hart Senate Office Building, 202-224-9167

The Library of Congress also has its own job board and employment information on its website (**www.loc.gov/hr/employment/index.php**). Interested applicants can submit their résumé and cover letter through the Library of Congress website. The Library of Congress has positions open for applicants new to the federal government, current government employees, and library employees. Résumés and cover letters can each be created separately and then attached to an online application.

Legislative and local or regional

Federal legislative positions are handled through each individual Congressional representative's office regardless of the physical location of the job. This means that local and regional office positions are still hired through the same process as described in the previous section and can be searched for through the same website as listed in the previous section. Jobs in local and regional offices include a wide variety of office positions and public relations positions. These legislative positions represent the federal government. They are just as competitive and should be treated with the same seriousness as jobs in Washington, D.C. Résumés and cover letters should be created with utmost professionalism. It is also important to note that many legislative positions are attached to specific members of Congress. This means that if the Congressional representative leaves office, his or her staff might be replaced. There are also jobs connected to specific offices, such as the Government Accountability Office or the General Accounting Office.

U.S. Postal Service

The U.S. Postal Service has its own system of hiring that is separate from the federal government. It is important to note that while President Obama eliminated the written essay portion of federal job applications in May 2010, most postal positions still require a written exam. There are five basic steps to applying for a position with the U.S. Postal Service.

1. **Find a job opening that fits you.** The Postal Service has positions that are full-time, part-time, and casual/temporary. Casual/temporary positions are positions offered June through December when the Postal Service is at its busiest time. Casual/temporary employees are not required to take the postal exam, but if they work more than 180 days, they are eligible to take the exam and fill a full-time permanent position. Casual/temporary employees are required to work long hours, often seven days a week during the Post Office's busiest times. Most applicants are hired in as casual or part-time and then move up to full-time. Exceptions to this include janitorial staff. There are roughly 2,000 types of jobs within the Postal Service, and

there are approximately 40,000 new employees hired every year to replenish the employees who quit, are fired, or retire.

2. **Research the position to have a full understanding of what is required and how to apply.** If the position does not require a written exam, you can skip to step five. Each position can be researched through the Postal Service website (**www.usps.com/employment**), which is where open positions are listed. It is important to check whether the position requires the completion of the 473 Battery Exam. The 473 Battery Exam is a five-part test, which has to be completed at an approved testing center at a designated time. This timed exam tests the applicants' ability to perform basic functions that will be required of them once they are hired. Section one of the exam tests the applicant's ability to look at two addresses and determine whether they are the same. Section two assesses the applicant's ability to identify needed information to complete a form. Section three tests the applicant's ability to use proper codes to assign to addresses. Section four verifies the applicant's ability to memorize address codes. Section five is based on the applicant's past experiences and job-related characteristics.

3. **Complete the job application.** Applicants can fill out an application, which can be obtained through the U.S. Postal Service website or through a District Postal Office. Qualified applicants will be contacted via e-mail with information on what they need to do next. If the next step includes an assessment, such as the 473 Battery Exam, the applicant will receive a login and password that will allow them access to the scheduling website.

4. **Study for the 473 Battery Exam.** The 473 Battery Exam does require the applicant to study. There is a study guide available through Amazon.com that will provide the applicant with all the postal codes he or she needs to have memorized prior to the exam. The study guide is titled *Post Office Jobs: Explore and Find Jobs, Prepare for the 473 Postal Exam, and Locate ALL Job Opportunities.*

CHAPTER 4

Finding Help Through the Internet

Years ago, people had to go to the local pharmacy for their prescriptions, the grocery store for food, the bank, the post office, and still another store for clothes. Running errands was an all-day event. Then, discount stores such as Kmart® and Walmart started expanding their line of products. They began building bigger stores and calling them "super." Now customers can go to a Super Walmart for all their shopping needs. They can do their banking, buy stamps, and even visit the eye doctor while buying groceries and a new outfit for the weekend.

The USAJOBS website is similar to a "super" store. Individuals interested in working for the federal government can go to this website to search for jobs; create a résumé; apply for jobs; gain helpful information on the hiring process, federal statistics and historical information; and creating a résumé. It is the one-stop shop for federal employment. Even if a job application is actually submitted through a different website, the USAJOBS website will provide the job description and a link to the proper website.

Although the USAJOBS website is the most used and the most popular, other websites are available that potential applicants can go to in search of job openings. One such website is Avue® Central (**www.avuecentral.com**), which will be discussed further in this chapter. Many agencies also list job openings on their website, so if you know which agency you want to work for, you can go directly to their website. It is also important to remember that the OPM website can answer your specific questions. The Internet provides a vast number of resources for perspective federal employees.

USAJOBS.GOV — THE NO. 1 STOP FOR FEDERAL JOBS

Although there are other federal job search websites one can search, the USAJOBS website is the most complete listing of federal job openings. Even agencies that offer job openings on their own websites or other web-sites also list them on the USAJOBS website. The jobs can be searched using a variety of different filters, which enable prospective applicants to refine their job search. The following list shows ways to filter jobs through an advance job search on the USAJOBS website:

- **Salary:** You can choose the salary range you are looking for, and the search will only compile positions within that range.

- **Grade:** The grade dictates your level of experience and education. You can limit your search to only certain grade positions.

- **Occupation:** For the occupation filter, you can choose the exact position you want, and the website will search for open positions in that occupation.

- **Agency:** If there is one specific agency you want to work for, you can search by agency.

- **Student jobs:** This filter will search for only jobs that are open to college students, which will cover internships.

- **Senior executive jobs:** This search filter is for current federal employees who are either looking to promote into the senior executive level or who are already senior executives looking for a new job or transfer.

- **Posting date:** You can search by the date the job was posted. This is helpful if you want to look for the most current jobs. It is also helpful if you know of a position that was posted on a certain date, and you want to find it.

- **Work schedule:** This filter allows you to look for only full-time, part-time, or positions with flexible schedules.

- **Tenure:** This filter will search for jobs in which tenure is available.

- **Exclusions:** This enables you to eliminate certain aspects you do not want, such as jobs open nationwide, and job postings that are more than 30 days old. If you regularly check the job postings, excluding jobs that are more than 30 days old will save you the time of reviewing job descriptions that you have already looked over.

Among some of the many resources this website offers applicants, it has an extensive information section, which can answer a majority of an applicant's general questions. There are sections of information specifically for veterans and applicants with disabilities, as well as student applicants and other special groups. The general information section includes information covering the benefits of working for the federal government, and the application process used by government agencies. The USAJOBS website also provides links to other relevant websites in each job description. This includes links to the OPM and agency websites.

On May 11, 2010, President Obama issued the Presidential Memorandum on Improving the Federal Recruitment and Hiring Process, which dictates that applicants should be able to receive notifications through the USA-JOBS website regarding the status of their application at key stages during the application process. Once this improvement is implemented, the USA-

JOBS website will become even more instrumental in the hiring process, and it will aid prospective applicants beyond submitting their résumés by allowing them to monitor their application status.

When you log onto the USAJOBS website, you will see a link for "First Time Visitors" below the large blue "Search Jobs" button. Click on "First Time Visitors." The page you will be directed to will give you three options: "Create an Account," "Be Informed," and "Look for a Job." Click on the "Be Informed" button to get to the information section. This link will take you to a page called "Info Center." The information on the page is separated into two main categories: "Browse Advice On" and "Special Info For." The second category will be covered in detail later in this chapter. The "Browse Advice On" section is separated into three additional categories, each of which will lead you to different information. The first category is organized in the following format:

1. Using USAJOBS

   • Tutorials
   • The job search
   • Using keywords to maximize your search results
   • Security center

2. Federal Employment

   • General
   • New to federal service
   • Current or returning federal employees

3. Applying for a federal job

   • Hiring reform
   • Tips on applying
   • Targeted occupations
   • Supplemental forms

Toward the bottom of the page is a link to frequently asked questions (FAQ). There are 102 FAQs listed in this section. Below the FAQ section is a "Contact Us" option in case you have a question that was not answered in the FAQ section.

The supplemental forms section under "Applying for a Federal Job" will provide you with links to many of the forms, which could be required in a job description. These include:

- SF15 — Application for 10-point Veterans Preference
- 1203-FX Qualifications and Availability, Form C supplemental
- OF-612 — Optional Application for Federal Employment
- Astronaut Applicant Supplemental Forms
- Department of Homeland Security — I-9 Employment Eligibility Verification Form
- Department of Veterans Affairs Application Forms
- Defense Logistics Agency and Defense Contract Management Agency's Automated Staffing Program (ASP)
- Department of the Interior — Applicant Background Survey form, DI-1935 B
- Federal Aviation Administration (FAA) Agency Forms
- Resumix — one-page supplemental data sheet

This page will also provide links to forms, which are supplied through OPM, as well as optional and standard forms that will apply to specific positions or situations. Several agencies and positions require specific forms to be filled out and submitted with the résumé. Any needed forms will be detailed in the job description.

What the site can do for you

The USAJOBS website can enable an applicant to set up an online profile and save search job search results. Job descriptions and résumés can also be saved within an applicant's online profile. This aids an applicant who might be applying for multiple positions. Applicant can keep an online profile after they have been hired by a federal agency. This allows them to search jobs whenever they want and keep their online résumé continually updated. This ability is essential for federal employees looking to move, transfer, or apply for a promotion. Federal employees still have to go through the application process if they are applying for another position within the federal government.

The USAJOBS website will help an applicant stay organized when applying for multiple positions at once. It can answer questions and provide an applicant with contact information when needed. Although the website also helps current federal employees, its simple design and format helps make the process easier for perspective federal employees. All the information is easy to find and written in plain language. The multiple site maps also help new users navigate the website and find the information they are looking for.

Current information about jobs

The USAJOBS website is continually updated and provides the most accurate and up-to-date information. If there is a change in a job posting, it will be immediately changed on the website. This will prevent you from applying for a job, only to find out the job listing changed after you saw it, you no longer qualify, or you missed an important element of the application packet. If you printed out a job description to use while preparing your application packet, it is important to look it up again before submitting your résumé and cover letter. This will enable you to be aware of any changes made to the job description after you printed it out.

Likewise, changes made to profiles or résumés are changed immediately after the applicant hits the "Save changes" button. Résumés do not need to be written all at once. An applicant can go back and work on the résumé as many times as he or she needs to. This also allows the applicant to update the résumé as a current job position changes, or he or she acquires an additional accomplishment. Every bit of information an applicant needs to successfully apply for a federal position will be supplied through the job description found on the USAJOBS website.

OTHER ONLINE RESOURCES

Although USAJOBS is an OPM-approved federal Web-based employment search portal, it is not the only source of information on federal employment, or the only website where individuals can search for federal jobs. Avue Central is USAJOBS' closest competitor. As of 2010, Avue Central is used by more than 25 different federal agencies; the Avue Central website (**www.avuecentral.com**) provides its own list of job openings, most of which are also listed on the USAJOBS website. If an applicant finds a job that is handled by Avue Central on the USAJOBS website, the applicant will be directed to the Avue Central website upon applying.

The Avue Central website offers a wide variety of employment and demographic information related to 28 of the top hiring agencies in the federal government. The website provides applicants with the number of available jobs within these agencies by state. It also offers detailed employment information for the following federal agencies:

- Department of Agriculture
- Department of Commerce
- Department of Defense
- Department of the Air Force
- Department of the Army
- Department of the Navy
- Department of Education
- Department of Energy
- Department of Health and Human Services
- Department of Homeland Security
- Department of Housing and Urban Development
- Department of Interior
- Department of Justice
- Department of Labor
- Department of State
- Department of Transportation
- Department of Treasury
- Department of Veterans Affairs
- Agency for International Development

- Environmental Protection Agency
- General Services Administration
- National Aeronautics and Space Administration
- National Science Foundation
- Office of Personnel Management

- Small Business Administration
- Securities and Exchange Commission
- Smithsonian Institute
- Social Security Administration

In addition to agency specific information, Avue Central provides general information on federal employment, advantages of federal employment, tips on preparing the application packet, interviewing tips, pay scales, and a glossary of terms commonly used words in job descriptions.

Other websites that might be helpful for those seeking federal employment are the U.S. Army Civilian Personnel website (**http://cpol.army.mil**), Department of the Navy's Civilian Hiring and Recruitment website (**https://chart.donhr.navy.mil**), the Air Force Personnel Center website (**www.afpc.randolph.af.mil**), and the USA.gov website (**www.usa.gov/**), which provides information on all agencies within the government and current news topics. The Army, Navy, and Air Force Civilian Personnel websites are a combination of the OPM website and the USAJOBS website, but targeted specifically to prospective and current military civilian employees.

GUIDELINES FOR RÉSUMÉ WRITING AND COVER LETTERS

The USAJOBS website also provides applicants with position-specific guidelines for writing the résumé and cover letter. Some positions might state they do not want a cover letter. Others might list the specific information the hiring manager will be looking for in the cover letter. A position might specify a page limit for the résumé and cover letter or detail specific information they will be looking for in the résumé. The department hiring for the position determines specific guidelines for the résumé and cover letter, and they might be vastly different from one position to the next. The USAJOBS job description will also supply the applicant with the keywords they will need to write their résumé. Finding and using keywords will be addressed later in this chapter.

Under the information section, the USAJOBS website provides some general information an applicant should be aware of going into the application process for a federal job. An applicant who is serious about obtaining a position in the federal government should carefully review both the information section on the USAJOBS website as well as on the OPM website. Both provide keys to gaining federal employment and information regarding security clearances and benefits.

The information section for job seekers on the OPM website is divided into four categories, each listing multiple links to specific information. To get to the information section, log onto the OPM website (**www.opm.gov**), and then click on the link titled "Job Seekers." This will take you to the information page, and the information page is organized in the following manner:

1. Finding Federal Jobs

    - Recovery jobs
    - USAJOBS
    - Jobs in demand
    - Senior executive jobs
    - Job FAQs
    - Veteran's employment resources
    - Persons with disabilities

2. Career Opportunities

    - Federal career intern
    - Executive in residence

- Federal executive institute
- Intergovernmental personnel act mobility
- Detail and transfer to international organizations
- Career transition resources

3. Student Opportunities

- Student jobs
- Presidential management fellows
- Student educational employment
- Summer employment scholarship for service
- E-scholar

4. Benefits of Being a Federal Employee

- Benefits for new federal employees
- Retirement benefits
- Insurance programs
- Work-life enrichment

Some of these links will take you to information unique to OPM, and some of them will take you to pages on other websites such as the USA-JOBS website. Either way, the information provided is valuable in helping perspective federal employees find the information and job descriptions that apply to them. Knowing where to go for information will help an applicant save time when preparing to apply for a federal position.

Tips for career changers

If you are an experienced worker looking for a federal job, you are in good company. More than 40 percent of the people hired by the federal government last year were experienced workers over the age of 35. The following tips will help you to get credit for your expertise:

- **Estimate your GS level.** The federal government classifies positions according to the complexity of their job duties and their level of responsibility. People qualify for a given level based on education, experience, or a combination of both. The most common classification system is the General Schedule (GS). To find your GS level, estimate the level you qualify for based on education alone. If you also have relevant experience, your GS level will be higher than that. If you have had relevant managerial responsibilities or do complex work independently, you might qualify for a GS-12 or above. To be certain, read the job descriptions in vacancy announcements.

- **Understand job requirements.** Vacancy announcements often say that a worker needs experience equivalent to a particular GS level. A vacancy announcement at the GS-12 level, for example, might say that you need one year of experience at the GS-11 level. Some announcements give examples of what that experience could be. Others do not. The simplest way to know if you qualify for a job is to read the job duties. If the work described there is only slightly more complex or responsible than work you have done in the past, you might be eligible for the position. If some of the required experience for a job seems unique to the federal government, explore further by calling the agency or the contact person for the position. You might learn that your private-sector experience meets the requirement.

- **Be flexible about titles.** If you want to be a manager or supervisor, do not limit yourself to openings with those words in the job title. Jobs with widely varying levels of responsibility are often listed under the same title.

- **Be specific about past experience.** Human resources managers will study the details of your application to decide if you qualify for a job. They will compare your past work to the types of tasks performed at different GS levels. Managers will pay close attention to the amount of time you spent in each job. They usually estimate exactly how many months or years you have done each major job task. When creating a résumé or writing statements about your skills, show your level of expertise by explaining whom you reported to or worked with and how your work was used.

- **Explain past job titles.** Use job titles that clearly describe what you did. You might want to put the equivalent federal title in parentheses next to your actual job titles.

- **Consider Senior Executive Service.** Finally, if you have substantial experience in high-level leadership positions, you might qualify for the Senior Executive Service (SES). SES positions require you to answer a set of standard questions about your leadership ability. A review board established by the U.S. Office of Personnel Management will certify your qualifications based on your answers and your experience. For more information, see **www.opm.gov/ses** or call (202) 606-1800.

TIPS AND INFORMATION ON THE INTERVIEWING PROCESS

The USAJOBS website provides valuable information regarding the federal hiring process, including the interview. When you go to the USAJOBS home page, click on "First Time Visitors." Then click on the large button that says, "Be Informed." This will direct you to the information section of the website. This page contains a great deal of information. Click on "Applying for a Federal Job," and a list of topics will appear to the right. Click on "Tips on Applying," and that will give you three options:

1. Résumé and application tips, which includes paying attention to detail, being concise, and using numbered lists to present information

2. Interviewing tips, which includes dressing the part, maintaining a positive attitude, and remembering to write a thank-you letter following the interview

3. Ten tips for letting federal employers know your worth, which includes using your words wisely, keeping sentences short and concise, using subheadings and short paragraphs, including time

frames for past positions, highlighting leadership positions, and using examples to highlight past experiences

Each of these three sections is filled with ideas and information that increase your chances of being hired into a federal position. The second section on interviewing tips provides four solid ideas, which can help an applicant preparing for an interview.

The USAJOBS website recommends you:

1. Develop and practice a one-minute résumé
2. Be positive
3. Dress the part
4. Write a thank-you letter following the interview

Applicants can find additional tips on interviewing on the Avue Central website (**www.avuecentral.com**). Go to the Avue Central home page. Then, click on the "Federal Hiring Tools" button, which will be at the top of the page. This will take you to a general information page, with options on the right side of the screen. Click on the option that says "Interviewing Skills." This will take you to information regarding how to make the most of an interview for a federal job. Avue Central's tips center around: 1. establishing interview objectives and 2. making a good first impression.

ADDRESSING PARTICULAR CIRCUMSTANCES SUCH AS VETERANS OR FORMER MILITARY STATUS

Veterans are given preferential status when applying for a federal position. In order to be considered a veteran officially, one must serve at least 90 days during wartime or at least 180 days during peacetime and be released honorably. When you visit the USAJOBS website, click on "Veterans," which will be located directly below "Why Work for America?" You will be directed to another page with a brief description of the federal government's desire to hire veterans and a link to another website. Click on the link, and you will be directed to the Feds Hire Vets website (**www.fedshirevets.gov**). This website was specifically created to help veterans navigate the federal hiring process. On this website, you will find current news and information affecting veterans, information about the website, and a job search option. In addition, this website provides an agency directory with specific names and contact information of individuals within each agency who are available to help veterans obtain a federal job. The federal government is eager to hire veterans, which is why veterans are given preferred status. Establishing your veteran status will significantly increase your chances of obtaining federal employment, regardless of the position or agency. This is also why most agencies have contact people available to assist veterans through the application process. All veterans, as well as people with disabilities, current and former federal employees, and returning Peace Corps volunteers are given non-competitive status. This means they are considered before candidates without non-competitive status.

When you go to the information center page on the USAJOBS website, you will find links to pages of information for students and persons with disabilities, in addition to information for veterans. When you click on the link for individuals with disabilities, you will be able to go an information page dedicated to information for individuals with disabilities who want to work for the federal government. There is also a listing of job opportunities for individuals with disabilities. If you click on the link for "Students," you will be given seven options:

- Students information page
- Federal jobs by college major
- Student educational employment programs (STEP/SCEP)
- Student career experience (SCEP)
- Internships
- Summer employment
- Volunteer service

Veterans should also click on "First Time Visitor" on the main page of the USAJOBS website. This will direct you to a screen that provides three options. The second option is "Be informed." Click on that option, and you will be taken to a page with categories of information. Scroll down past the box, and you will find a link to "Frequently Asked Questions." Click on this option, and scroll through the questions. Several questions deal specifically with veterans who are applying for a federal position. This section includes questions regarding veterans preference, non-competitive status, what forms are required for veterans, and where those forms can be found. This section might be able to provide you with needed information before you contact someone for assistance.

Executive Order
Employment of Veterans in the Federal Government
November 9, 2009

President Obama publicly recognizes the wide variety of skills possessed by veterans, which they gained through their military development and training. Veterans also have a recognized motivation for public service and are ideal candidates for federal employment. With this in mind, President Obama has decided to establish the Interagency Council on Veterans Employment (Council). The council will be run by OPM, the Secretary of Labor, and the Secretary of Veterans Affairs.

The mission of the council will be to: 1. assist the President and OPM to coordinate and develop a government-wide initiative to increase the employment of veterans, 2. serve as a national forum to promote veterans' employment opportunities in the executive branch, and 3. to establish performance and evaluation methods to determine the effectiveness of the Veterans Employment Initiative.

The executive order includes the following list of actions, which will be performed in order to accomplish the overall goal of increase federal employment of veterans:

1. Develop agency-specific plans to promote employment of veterans

2. Within 120 days of this order, create a Veterans Employment Program Office within each agency, which will head up veteran recruitment and training programs

3. Provide mandatory annual training for human resources personnel on veterans' employment needs

4. Identify key occupations that veterans can fill with addition training or job counseling

5. Work with the Department of Defense and Veterans Affairs to increase the technology available to accommodate veterans with disabilities

6. Develop a government-wide veteran's recruitment and employment strategy

7. Identify things agency leaders can be doing to increase veteran employment

8. Provide skills development for transitioning military service members and veterans

9. Market the federal government to transitioning military service members and veterans

10. Market the skills, experience, and training of transitioning military service men and veterans to Federal agencies

11. Break down and explain federal employment information for both veterans and hiring managers

12. Compile and post veteran hiring statistics on the OPM website

13. Provide workshops for military service personnel and veterans to provide information on federal employment opportunities, veterans' preference laws, special hiring authorities, and the federal hiring process

14. Assist transitioning service members and veterans in how to translate and explain their military skills, training, and experience in how it can be applied to a federal position

LINKS TO JOBS

The USAJOBS website provides a description for almost every job opening in the federal government despite the fact not all federal positions can be applied for through the USAJOBS website. For job applications located on other websites, the USAJOBS website will provide a link to the job application. For example, the USAJOBS website links to the Avue Central website. An applicant can also go to the USAJOBS website to get information about a position, and then go to the website of the hiring agency to learn more about the agency and the position.

HOW THIS SITE CAN HELP LAND YOU A FEDERAL JOB

Using the USAJOBS website will give an applicant an advantage over applicants who do not take advantage of the vast amount of information and resources available through the website. All of the information regarding the USAJOBS website thus far outlines all the reasons using this website provides an advantage for potential applicants. An applicant simply needs to register and create an account on the website and everything the USAJOBS website has to offer is free to its users. The site is a free resource to help future federal employees navigate through the hiring process.

The job descriptions provided on the USAJOBS website are often pages long, and they provide every bit of information an applicant will need. The website also provides links to other websites or documents the applicant might need to apply for the job. The website offers a résumé builder, which will be covered in the next section. The résumé builder is a great asset for applicants who have never written a federal résumé before.

RÉSUMÉ BUILDERS

Although the résumé builder feature on the USAJOBS website is one of the most popular options, it is not the only one. There are also the following resources, each of which are explained throughout this section:

- QuickHire® (explained later in this section)
- Avue Central (**www.avuecentral.com**)
- Civilian Personnel Online (CPOL) (**http://cpol.army.mil**)
- Department of the Navy's Civilian Hiring and Recruitment Tool (CHART) (**https://chart.donhr.navy.mil**)
- Air Force Personnel Center (**www.afpc.randolph.af.mil**)

The last three are military-specific. The Army uses CPOL, and the Navy uses CHART. Each résumé builder is slightly different, but they all have the same basic components and objectives. They will each walk an applicant through the process of creating a résumé for a federal position. Each résumé builder divides the total résumé into the needed sections and has the applicant work on one section at a time. At the end of the process, the résumé builder will format the résumé and allow the applicant to review and save it.

The USAJOBS résumé builder contains 12 sections for the applicant to fill out and is the most extensive of the résumé builder options. You will be able to access the résumé builder after creating your USAJOBS account. The 12 sections are as follows:

1. **Candidate information:** As the name suggests, this is where the applicant will provide all of his or her contact information, which will appear at the top of the completed résumé.

2. **Work experience:** In this section of the résumé builder, the applicant will provide information regarding his or her past work experience. This section can be tailored depending on the position being applied for, which will be discussed further. You can write about as many jobs as you wish, however, each job description will

be limited to 3,000 characters. You should focus on the jobs that are most relevant to the position you are applying for, especially if you have a long work history.

3. **Education:** This section will be brief. You can simply list the university or universities you have attended, your graduation date(s), and the degree(s) you earned. If you have partial coursework done for an advanced degree, it also can be listed in this section. Include the name of the university, the intended degree, and the number of completed credit hours.

4. **Relevant coursework, licensure, and certifications:** This section will allow the applicant to accomplish two goals. The first is to list all the licensures and certifications he or she has obtained. This determines the applicant's qualifications, but it also provides the agency with additional information regarding the applicant's career focus. The second goal of this section is to direct the hiring manager to coursework the applicant might have completed that is not reflected in their completed degree. For example, an applicant might have completed a year of communications coursework prior to switching majors and graduating with a degree in political science. This section is limited to 2,000 characters, so if the list of certifications and licensures is extensive, the applicant should narrow it down to those most relevant to the position for which he or she is applying.

5. **Job-related training:** This section is also limited to 2,000 characters and provides applicants with the opportunity to detail on-the-job training they received, which might not be reflected in their education or certifications.

6. **References:** This section can contain work-related references as well as personal references. Prior to submitting the résumé, an applicant should check the job description to determine whether there are any special instructions regarding the references. An agency might want a specific number of references or a specific combination.

For example, it might ask for two professional references and three personal, but non-related, references.

7. **Additional language skills:** This is where an applicant should list any languages he or she can speak, understand, or write. An applicant does not have to be fluent in order to include a language in this section. For example, if an applicant has a basic understanding of Spanish and can communicate, it should be included. Obviously, to be hired as a translator, an applicant needs to be fluent, but positions are available that give preferences to applicants who can simply communicate in a certain language.

8. **Affiliations:** Here, applicants can mention membership and activity in professional organizations.

9. **Professional publications:** If an applicant has been published in a professional or academic journal, he or she should provide the reference information for the article and publication. This section is limited to 2,000 characters, so only the most relevant articles should be included for applicants who have been published extensively.

10. **Additional information:** This part is slightly open-ended. It has a maximum of 22,000 characters for applicants to detail skills, honors, experience, or awards that were not covered in the previous sections.

11. **Availability:** This section will give the applicant a list of options, and they should check all that apply.

12. **Desired locations:** This is where applicants can list the cities and/or states they wish to be located in. This is particularly important if they are applying for an open and continuous position, or if they intend to make their résumé searchable. Open and continuous positions are those positions that can always be applied for. When submitting an application, an applicant requests the state or region he or she wishes to work in, and the application is only considered

after a position in that specific state or region becomes available. This will let recruiters and hiring managers know ahead of time which areas the applicant is willing to relocate to.

Another online résumé builder is QuickHire, which is owned by Monster. com®. Many federal agencies use QuickHire to collect and assess incoming résumés. Although the job will still be listed on the USAJOBS website, the résumé will be sent to the QuickHire website. QuickHire provides its own résumé builder, but it is substantially less extensive than the USAJOBS résumé builder. The QuickHire résumé builder has only five sections, which are as follows:

1. **User information:** This is where the applicant will provide all of his or her contact information.

2. **Citizenship:** Applicants use this section to verify or define the terms of their citizenship.

3. **Military information:** This is specifically designed for veterans looking for federal employment. This section allows veterans to verify their veteran status by submitting their military record and honorable discharge status.

4. **Work experience:** This section limits the character count to 16,000 characters for all work history, forcing applicants using this résumé builder to be very concise in their wording.

5. **Questions:** The fifth section is actually a set of 25 yes-or-no questions that the applicant will need to answer in order to complete the résumé.

The Avue Central website has its own résumé builder as well, which applicants can use when applying for a job listed on that website. The Avue Central résumé builder is comparable to the USAJOBS résumé builder. It has nine sections for the applicant to complete and allows the applicant to upload supporting documentation directly to the résumé. The ten sections in the résumé builder are as follows:

1. **Applicant information:** Applicant information will cover the applicant's contact information.

2. **Work history:** This section is limited to 4,000 characters, which again shows the need for applicants to be concise in the wording they use.

3. **Eligibilities:** This section allows the applicant to address specific eligibility requirements listed in the job description. For example, if the job description states that applicants should be willing to relocate, you can state your willingness to relocate in this section.

4. **References:** This section should detail the names and contact information of professional references.

5. **Educational background:** Degrees should be listed in this section, as well as contact information for colleges and universities attended.

6. **Relevant information:** This section should cover an applicant's relevant non-work experience. This can include specialized skills and volunteer work.

7. **Awards, community service, training, certifications, collateral duties, significant details:** This section combines multiple sections an applicant would find on the USAJOBS résumé builder. Because there are several items put into the same section, it is important for the applicant to organize the information in a logical manner.

8. **Other considerations:** This is where the applicant should detail their military service history, if applicable.

9. **Additional information:** This section allows the applicant to provide any information about themselves that they were not able to fit anywhere else in the résumé. Additional information can in-

clude personal hobbies or interests that could be associated with your ability to fulfill the position for which you are applying. This section could also be used to explain extended gaps in employment.

The Civilian Personnel Online (CPOL) résumé builder is available through the U.S. Army and designed for civilians applying for a position with the Army. According to the CPOL website, the Army employs approximately 250,000 civilians and is the largest employer within the Department of Defense. The CPOL website is another valuable resource for individuals seeking employment with the Army. It is a combination of the OPM website and the USAJOBS website and tailored specifically to civilian employment opportunities with the Army. Civilian employment openings for the Army will also appear on the USAJOBS website. The CPOL résumé builder has only four sections for an applicant to complete and is much more focused than the larger résumé builders offered by USAJOBS and Avue Central. The following sections are including in the CPOL résumé builder:

1. **Contact information:** This section should include full name, address, phone number, and e-mail.

2. **Work experience:** The CPOL résumé builder allows applicants just up to 12,000 characters for all their employment history. This is significantly less than the character count for the USAJOBS résumé builder.

3. **Education:** This entire section has a maximum of 2,000 characters. Because an applicant should provide their complete educational background, the relevant coursework will have to be chosen carefully to stay within the character limit.

4. **Additional information:** This section covers performance reviews and awards, licensures, and certifications. However, the entire section is a maximum of 6,000 characters, so it is important to select the certifications, licensures, and achievements that are the most relevant to the position for which you are applying.

The Department of the Navy's Civilian Hiring and Recruitment Tool (CHART) résumé builder is the Navy's version of the résumé builder for its civilian employment opportunities. According to the CHART website, the Navy is the top federal employer of veterans. The Navy offers a wide variety of civilian jobs, and the CHART website offers information, job listings, and the résumé builder for potential applicants. Job listings for civilian positions in the Navy are also listed on the USAJOBS website. The CHART résumé builder provides the following eight sections:

1. **Contact information:** Contact information should include full name, address, phone number, and e-mail.

2. **Eligibility:** Describing an applicant's eligibility refers directly back to the eligibility requirements established in the job description.

3. **Education:** The education section should include a list of all degrees earned, as well as each school attended.

4. **Work History:** The CHART résumé builder allows up to 7,500 characters in the work history section.

5. **Other work-related history:** This section is where an applicant can list their job-related training, licensures, and certifications, which will save space in the work history section.

6. **Performance rating, awards, honors, and recognitions:** This section only allows 1,500 characters. It is essential for applicants to only include the most important accolades and that they choose their wording extremely carefully.

7. **Other Information:** This section allows the applicant to provide any other information they feel will make them more appealing to the hiring manager.

8. **U.S. Military Service:** The Navy is the federal government's top employer of veterans. As a testament to its commitment to em-

ploying veterans, the Navy includes a special section in its résumé builder for applicants to detail their military history.

The Air Force Personnel Center résumé builder is provided through the Air Force Personnel Center website. This website is very similar to the CPOL site and the CHART site, but it is tailored to individuals interested in seeking civilian employment with the Air Force. The website provides the résumé builder, job listings, and general information regarding civilian employment, as well as continually updated news that might be of interest to civilian Air Force employees. The Air Force Personnel Center résumé builder is broken down into eight sections for applicants to fill out when creating their résumé. As you will see, the Air Force résumé builder has a very limited character count, which is important to keep in mind while choosing your wording. This résumé builder provides the following eight sections:

1. **Personal and contact information:** This section is where a full name, address, phone number, and e-mail should be provided.

2. **Summary of skills:** This section requires applicants to provide a list of skills, which can include Microsoft® PowerPoint®, payroll, small engine repair, etc. The list is limited to 1,500 characters, including spaces.

3. **Experience and employment history:** The Air Force résumé builder only allows applicants to write about up to six jobs and has a maximum character count of 1,500 characters.

4. **Licenses and certifications:** This section is limited to 300 characters and can be presented in the form of a list.

5. **Awards:** This section can also be presented as a list and is limited to 300 characters.

6. **Other information:** Like the other résumé builders, this section allows applicants to provide any information they feel is essential

for the hiring manager to know about them. Other information is limited to 300 characters.

7. **Education requirements:** An applicant should use this section to provide an outline of the educational background starting with the most recent.

8. **Supplemental information:** Here, applicants can provide support to the information supplied in the résumé. This can include copies of specialized training completion certificates.

How it can help you

Because most sections in résumé builders have a maximum number of characters allowed, and spaces count as characters, formatting is not as essential in online-created résumés. The human resources staff understands that space is limited. The character limit prevents applicants from writing too much, including unnecessary information, and forces the applicant to consider what is most important for the hiring manager to know. Choose words wisely and use an active voice.

The applicant will fill out each section as perfectly and completely as if they were simply writing his or her résumé. The résumé builder will then format the information into a résumé, which can be viewed online or printed out. Résumé builders also provide a spell check, much like the Microsoft Word spell check, but they will not catch all mistakes. Print the résumé and proofread it several times before submitting it with a job application. It is also highly recommended that you have a second person read over your résumé with a critical eye to offer an outside perspective and constructive suggestions. Often, individuals cannot properly proofread and edit their own writing because they are more likely to read what they think they wrote as opposed to what is actually written. In addition, a third person will allow you to see whether you used plain language to make it understandable to someone not already in your given profession. Using plain language in a résumé and cover letter is always important because you cannot be sure who will be reading them. Using words or acronyms that are unfamiliar to the reader will lessen the importance of what was written.

Another benefit to using the résumé builder is that it prevents the applicant from forgetting to add things to their résumé. Because every topic of information has its own section to be completed, it is less likely that applicants will forget to include their achievements because they are concentrating on their work history. Writing the résumé in sections also prevents the applicant from focusing on the overall length of the résumé, which can become distracting. The résumé builder program will prevent an applicant from writing a résumé that is too long.

CASE STUDY: USING THE USAJOBS RÉSUMÉ BUILDER

Dustin Parker
Educational aid
Federal Student Aid

I had the opportunity to use the USAJOBS website, as well as its résumé builder, and I would recommend both to individuals interested in working for the federal government. The résumé builder streamlines the entire process, which can save a great deal of time. When deciding what to include in the résumé, I would recommend risking too much information rather than not enough. I know the general recommendation is to write short résumés, but federal job are very competitive, and it is sometimes hard to determine which set of skills the hiring manager will be looking for.

My final résumé was about five pages long when I started, but the résumé builder format adds some length. It probably would have been three pages or a little over three pages if I had tried to format it myself. I am not saying I would discourage perspective applicants from writing their résumés on their own; I just think if the tools are available, you might as well use them.

As for cover letters, I think it is most important to be yourself. Some of the cover letters I have seen were so formal, it was hard to get a feel for the person who wrote it. Obviously, the letters still have to be professional, but applicants should not be afraid to tell the hiring manager why they are the best applicant for the position. Confidence is very important when applying for a federal position.

Uploading your résumé

Uploading your résumé to an online application is a simple process and can be completed quickly. However, it is important that you are 100 percent confident about your résumé before it is uploaded. Although you can always go back to a saved résumé and make changes through the résumé builder, you cannot make changes once it has been submitted to a human resources department for consideration.

The USAJOBS website allows you to keep up to five résumés saved to your online profile. This will allow you to save résumés that are tailored to specific positions. Make sure you send the correct résumé when applying for a position — always double-check what you are doing before you submit anything to a human resources department. A simple mistake can bar you from getting the perfect federal job.

It is also important to note that although the résumé builders are great resources, you are not required to use them. The USAJOBS website will allow you to upload résumés written in a different program, such as Microsoft Word, to your online profile if you prefer. Then, when you are ready to apply for a position, go to your online profile and attach the résumé you want to use. *The information on crafting the perfect résumé, which will be discussed in Chapter 6, can be applied to résumés written in a résumé builder or independently.*

Why you should upload your résumé before applying for a position

There are two reasons you should upload your résumé prior to actually applying for a federal position online. Having the résumé uploaded and ready to go prior to applying for a federal position will decrease your chances of making a mistake. If you sit down to apply for the job and quickly fill in each section of the résumé builder, you will rush through the process and not take the time to choose your words and proofread the final draft carefully. Each résumé builder allows you to print out the completed résumé so you can see how it will look to the hiring manager. Take advantage of the opportunity to make your résumé as perfect as possible. Although the perfect résumé will not guarantee you the position you are applying for, it will greatly increase your chances of being hired. Having your résumé prepared and uploaded will make you ready for any unexpected opportunities that might arise.

Spending time to prepare beforehand will be a major time-saver

Like most things in life, preparation is the key to success when applying for a federal job. Reading this book is an excellent way to prepare for the federal hiring process. Attention to detail is an enduring theme considered by human resources staff and hiring managers when reviewing application packets. They expect everything submitted to have perfect spelling and grammar. Every item should follow the instructions laid out in the job description exactly and should be submitted within the time frame indicated in the job description.

Looking for the right job opening to fit your unique background and work experience takes time and requires a careful search using specific filters and keywords. It also requires reading through several job descriptions, many of which will not be the right position for you. Once you find a handful of job openings you think you might apply for, taking the time to print out the job descriptions will allow you to study them at your own pace. You can highlight items and make notes regarding keywords and phrases. Doing this now will help you when you sit down to write your résumé and cover letter.

Writing the résumé and cover letter, which will be covered in detail in Chapter 6 and Chapter 7, should take a good amount of time. Everything you write should be carefully considered, keeping in mind all the information in the job description. Each sentence should be well thought out and grammatically flawless. The perfect résumé and cover letter are a combination of perfect elements. If one element is off, both the résumé and cover letter suffer, which will affect your chances of gaining federal employment.

How to tweak your résumé once you find the right job

In general, the first résumé you write should be a generic description of your education, work history, skills, etc. Although the information will be broad, it should still be perfect in word choice, grammar, and spelling. Preparing a basic résumé to have on hand will save you the time and energy of looking up dates of previous employment, names, and reference contact information for every job for which you apply. In addition, a generic résumé will save you the time of rewriting the résumé each time you apply for a job because not all the information will need to be modified. Finally, it will prevent you from forgetting to change an element of the résumé that was tailored for a job for which you previously applied.

Once you have your basic résumé created and perfected, start looking for the positions for which you want to apply. Read over the job description carefully, and then look for things in your own work history that are applicable to the position. This might involve changing information in the basic résumé, adding information, or changing the order of the information listed. For example, for each job you apply for, awards and achievements should be listed in order of relevance to the position. The same goes for your work history. Here is an example: Suppose you had a job in sales, which involved meeting with customers, closing the deal, following up with customers to ensure satisfaction, recruiting and training new sales associates, and organizing monthly sales training meetings. If you are applying for a job that will involve training staff, then you want to list the training and planning monthly training meetings first. Those two elements of your previous job in sales should contain the most detail and be emphasized over the sales portion of your job.

CHAPTER 5

What You Need to Know About Writing the Perfect Federal Résumé and Cover Letter

S o far, we have looked at a variety of different factors that will impact both your decision to work for the federal government and your ability to obtain a job with the federal government. The focus thus far has been on the background information, job descriptions, and information specific to working and applying for the federal government. This chapter will cover the many differences between federal and private sector résumés. You will see the differences in format, presentation, and content that the human resources staff and hiring manager will expect to see when looking at résumés for an open position. In addition, this chapter will provide examples of the differences between federal and private sector résumés.

IMPROVING YOUR CHANCES OF BEING HIRED WITH THE PERFECT RÉSUMÉ

The résumé gives the federal hiring manager his or her first impression of the applicants. Depending on the quality of the résumé, it can give a positive first impression and entice the hiring manager to call the applicant in for an interview, or it can impart a negative impression, compelling the hiring manager to discard the résumé. A very poor quality résumé will be discarded before the hiring manager even has a chance to review it.

The perfect résumé will improve your chances of being hired for a federal position by demonstrating to the hiring manager that you are uniquely qualified for the open position. A perfect résumé will also show the hiring manager your superior written communication skills and professionalism. The perfect résumé will accomplish two things. First, it will lead to an interview with the hiring manager, which will be your opportunity to seal the deal. Second, it will put you at the top of the list among applicants being interviewed. The perfect résumé will show the hiring manager that you are more than qualified for the position.

CASE STUDY:
SIMPLE THINGS YOU CAN DO
TO IMPROVE YOUR CHANCES
OF BEING HIRED

Sara Hartmann
Human resources staff
Federal Emergency Management Agency

I have been working for the Federal Emergency Management Agency for more than 15 years, which has given me the opportunity to review countless application packets sent in by prospective employees. Although I do not make the decision when it comes to who is actually hired, I do review the résumé and application packets to ensure that all the needed credentials are there and the applicant followed the instructions in the job description.

Some problems I have encountered on more than one occasion, I would recommend applicants avoid.

The first is not following the instructions provided. I always feel badly when this happens, but if an application was not submitted properly with all the requested material, it does not get forwarded to the hiring manager. It is lost in the first round of eliminations. Another common problem is applicants not reading the qualifications for the job. If an applicant does not fit the basic qualifications for the position, their information does not get forwarded either. I hate applicants to waste time assembling an application packet for a position they are not qualified for.

Finally, the last mistake I see is applicants who submit a plain, generic résumé that lacks information pertaining to the open position. It is important that the résumé reflects the applicant's ability to fulfill the needs of the position being applied for. The hiring manager is not impressed by résumés that could have just as easily been used to apply for a job at the local mall. The competition for these positions is sometimes fierce, and generic résumés will be discarded when compared to the extensive position-specific résumés.

OVERVIEW OF DIFFERENCES BETWEEN A FEDERAL RÉSUMÉ AND A PRIVATE-SECTOR RÉSUMÉ

Although all résumés should highlight an applicant's skills and abilities, there are differences between a federal and private sector résumé. The following table points out some of the differences between the two.

The Federal Résumé	The Private Sector Résumé
Objective is not required	Objective is expected
The customer base is tax payers, as well as internal.	Stakeholders comprise the customer base.
Agency provides a program or service	Company provides a product or service.
Can be more than two pages	One to two pages in length is expected

The Federal Résumé	The Private Sector Résumé
Work descriptions should be highly detailed.	Work descriptions can be brief.
Traditional format is expected.	Creative or graphic formats are acceptable.
Keywords are essential.	Keywords are incidental.

The following two résumés demonstrate many of the differences between private sector and federal résumés. The first résumé — an example of a federal résumé — provides a detailed account of the applicant's qualifications and professional experience, which is given greater emphasis than the other information contained in the résumé. The second résumé — an example of a private sector résumé — provides brief and detail-lacking explanations of job responsibilities. The first résumé is considerably longer than the second, and the most important information is provided first. The first résumé also uses a wide variety of possible keywords, while the second résumé relies on basic language. Finally, the first résumé provides related information regarding professional associations and volunteer activities.

Résumé Sample 1

SARA WHITE
1230 Boulevard Street • City, State ZIP • (123) 456-7890
myemail@hotmail.com

SUMMARY OF QUALIFICATIONS

Highly organized, efficient writer with experience in technical writing, narratives, creative writing, corporate communications, and Web-based media; diversified background includes public relations, marketing, human resources, administration, songwriting, and international experience

- Takes initiative to actively pursue a variety of projects and takes pride in producing quality work that adheres to clients' requirements for content, tone, and length.

- Prioritizes multiple tasks effectively in order to meet strict deadlines; makes extra effort to finish projects ahead of schedule to exceed publishers' expectations and facilitate publication while delivering superior quality.

- Draws on experience gained living abroad to interact easily with people from various countries and cultures.

- Proficient in Word, Excel®, PowerPoint, Outlook®, PeopleSoft®, Access®, Publisher, Works, Resumix, and Explorer; familiar with AP style; types 75 words per minute.

EDUCATION

B.A., Journalism, Rutgers University, New Brunswick, New Jersey   1992
    Graduated with Honors; Phi Eta Sigma National Honor Society;
    Golden Key National Honor Society

PROFESSIONAL EXPERIENCE

Writing and Communications

- Wrote stories, took photos, and contributed ideas for layout of World-Com's 20-page magazine-style employee publication with approximately 500 readers, distributed on monthly basis.

  o Interviewed employees in government markets sector, developed articles about issues in that sector and biographies of established employees, and introduced new team members through biographical sketches.

  o Interacted heavily with numerous employees at many levels; planned future articles proactively in order to avoid deadline crunches.

  o Collaborated with graphic designer to refine layout and select cover and interior photos.

- Created user documentation for specialized software applications developed for large-scale organizations such as Starbucks Coffee® Company, Zurn®, and GE® Plastics; wrote, edited, proofread, and evaluated functional test plans for quality assurance.

- Spearheaded fund-raising for animal shelter faced with closing due to noise complaints; wrote news articles about shelter and managed public relations activities, helping to generate enough money for construction of sound wall.

- Developed, edited, and assembled literature about company history, mission, benefits, and policy; finished compilation was included in employee packets and handbooks.

rched, interviewed, wrote, and edited stories for Lifestyle section
ndsor Heights Herald under umbrella of Packet Publications; focused
on community and human interest topics.

- Commissioned by Midwest Publishing to write summations and reviews for three nonfiction books.

- Composed numerous song lyrics, leading to publication of several songs; original song "I Don't" received airplay on independent Florida radio station Country Bear.

- Wrote theatre reviews for **www.theatremonkey.com** on shows at West End in London; reviewed hotels for **www.tripadvisor.com**; developed restaurant critiques for **www.london-eating.co.uk**.

- Documented processes and procedures followed by HR department at Raytheon®; requested to write guidelines explaining internal and external employee transfer processes for distribution to HR company wide.

- Reduced printing costs by 25 percent for WorldCom's monthly publication by identifying prospective vendors, obtaining bids, and negotiating discounts and price reductions.

- Taped live readings of adult and children's literature through nonprofit organization helping blind individuals.

Administration

- Supported executives and project leaders through researching, scheduling, correspondence, logistics management, travel arrangements, expense account administration, file maintenance, and dictation.

- Restructured filing system to improve organization and accessibility; created and maintained personnel files.

- Processed payroll, completed accounts payable and receivable, generated reports, and created spreadsheets.

- Earned Raytheon's Achievement Award for Outstanding Performance for contributions toward reducing turnover and employee disconnect and improving organization within department.

- Recorded staff meeting minutes and circulated documents to department personnel.

- Researched and analyzed overdue accounts in settlements department of global phone services corporation.

- Assisted marketing team with preparations for trade shows.

Human Resources

- Established processes to be followed when handling company transfers; created and delivered presentation to HR and staffing departments and served as point of contact for transfer process.

- Initiated and maintained documented procedures of HR personnel to improve departmental workflow.

- Engaged in full life-cycle staffing for HR department, interviewing up to 10 candidates each day.

- Wrote and updated job descriptions, tracked résumé flow, verified candidates' education and references, and maintained database of prospective employees.

- Prescreened candidates, scheduled interviews, and generated sign-on bonus repayment agreements, offer letters, and no-interest letters.

- Compiled and distributed welcome packets, facilitated orientation class for new employees, and entered data into system using People-Soft and Resumix.

EMPLOYMENT HISTORY

Freelance Writer & Songwriter, United Kingdom   **2002-Present**

Raytheon, Falls Church, Virginia   **2001**
  Senior Human Resources Associate

Contract Employment, various locations in New Jersey,
and Virginia   **1993-1994, 1997-2000**
  Human Resources/Administrative Assistant

MCI WorldCom, McLean, Virginia   **2000**
  Communications Specialist

IMI/Palarco, Marlton, New Jersey   **1998**
  Technical Writer/Executive Assistant

The Packet Publications, Hightstown, New Jersey   **1996**
  Editorial Assistant/Reporter for Lifestyle Section

American List Counsel, Princeton, New Jersey   1994-1995
    Marketing Assistant

MFG Systems, Somerset, New Jersey   1992-1993
    Office Manager

VOLUNTEER EXPERIENCE

South Hook LNG Terminal Company, Milford Haven, Wales   2002-2008
    Personal Assistant, Southampton and London, England;
    Haverfordwest, Wales; and Houston, Texas

SAVE Animal Shelter, Princeton, New Jersey   1996
    Public Relations/Animal Caretaker

New Jersey Home for Disabled Soldiers, Menlo Park, New Jersey 1985-1996
    Recreation Assistant

Guiding Eyes for the Blind, Paris, France   1995
    Reader, Books on Tape

CERTIFICATION AND ASSOCIATIONS

CLAiT Level I Certification, Haverfordwest, Wales   2007

Guild of International Songwriters and Composers,
London, United Kingdom   2002-2008

Nashville Songwriters Association International

Résumé Sample 2

Juanite Holleran
1234 Boulevard Street
City, State, ZIP
123-456-7890

EDUCATION

Lee University, Cleveland, Tennessee, 1992-1994
Obtained a certification to teach elementary education and secondary education
with a concentration in English

University of Baltimore, Baltimore, Maryland, 1988-1990
Bachelor of Arts Degree in Jurisprudence, cum laude

The Hagerstown Business College, Hagerstown, Maryland, 1986-1988
Associate of Arts Degree, Legal Assistant

EMPLOYMENT

Correspondent, *The Dominion Post*, Morgantown, West Virginia,
September 2007-present
Write articles as assigned.

English Teacher, Board of Education of Allegany County, Cumberland, Maryland,
2004-2006
Taught 9th and 10th grade English classes.

English Teacher, Alldredge Academy, Davis, West Virginia, 2003-2003
Taught 9th-12th grade English to at-risk youth in a therapeutic wilderness setting.

English Instructor, Garrett College, McHenry, Maryland, 2002-2003
Taught developmental grammar and poetry classes; worked in writing center;
taught for spring writer's conferences; mentored and tutored students.

Artist in Education/Poet-in-Residence, Garrett County Arts Council, McHenry,
Maryland, 1999-2002
Taught poetry workshops; created and edited a literary and art magazine for
young people titled *Paper Flowers*; served on editorial board of *Ginseng* literary
magazine.

Researcher/Writer, Church of God World Missions, Cleveland, Tennessee, 1992-1994
Researched and wrote about the activities of missionaries in the Caribbean and
South America for a history book.

Claims Examiner, Maryland Department of Labor and Licensing, Oakland,
Maryland, 1990-1992
Determined claimants' eligibility for unemployment benefits; wrote
determinations based on unemployment insurance laws.

Paralegal, Allen, Thieblot & Alexander, Baltimore, Maryland, 1988-1990
Worked in asbestos litigation; went to courthouses for filing and
retrieving documents.

Legal Assistant, Martin Palmer, Attorney, Hagerstown, Maryland, 1986-1988
Worked on constitutional law reform; performed some secretarial work.

Legal Assistant Intern, Snyder & Benjamin, Hagerstown, Maryland, 1987
Worked on real estate titles; assisted in some criminal cases.

PUBLICATIONS

Ginseng, Welter, The Torch, Serving From the Ladle: A Collection of Poetry, Lewis Stemple: Art & Poetry, Ocean, The Charleston Gazette

OF NOTE

Exhibitor, Garrett College Art Gallery, McHenry, Maryland, 2001
Displayed with various artists artwork for my poetry collection titled *Serving From the Ladle.*

Exhibitor, Aurora Area Historical Society, Aurora, West Virginia, 2002
Worked with West Virginia Endowment for the Arts on a grassroots-based art project; led elementary students in creating poetry for the artwork of celebrated artist, Lewis Stemple for a poetry book, art show, and poetry reading by the children.

Nominated for Poet Laureate for the State of Maryland.

REFERENCES

Available upon request

Presentation is the same

Federal résumés are more detailed than private sector résumés. The federal hiring manager wants to know more about an applicant's work experience with significantly more detailed information. A federal résumé is expected to be longer than a private sector résumé, but it should not be overly wordy or too long. The federal résumé is less focused on visual appeal and more on content. A private sector résumé is typically a list of job responsibilities, while a federal résumé can describe them in paragraph form. The following is an example of a résumé written in paragraph form. Although this résumé would be better if it contained more specific information regarding achievements and responsibilities, it is well organized and easy to read.

Susan Mathis

Street Address
City, State ZIP
Home Phone: 000-000-0000
Cell Phone: 000-000-0000
Social Security Number
U.S. Citizen
Position applying for

Qualifications

Throughout the past 12 years, my knowledge and experience vastly increased within the field of journalism. Throughout my history with the Hagadone Corporation, I tackled a variety of journalistic and management challenges daily. My journalism career includes a wide range of topics, such as a series of stories about the Canadian response to Sept. 11, 2001, which were published in the November 2001 issue of *Idaho Magazine* and requested for use by the Idaho Department of Commerce to promote tourism in North Idaho. Several of my articles on domestic violence continue to be published on the State of Idaho website on this subject. My published articles also include numerous pieces on local murders, child molestation, sex offenders, accidents, elections, school board issues, local businesses, human interest, kids, community events, natural resources, timber industry, water issues, drug related stories, etc. With 5 ½ years experience as a managing editor of two weekly newspapers, an online newspaper, and coeditor of a professional publication of the multi-billion dollar industry of struggling teens, I believe I have a solid foundation of knowledge and expertise to share with any type of publication. I also spent one year as editor-in-chief of my college newspaper. I directly supervised five staff persons including reporters. I deliver not only management experience, but also thoroughly investigated, fair, and unbiased stories that are always ready on or before deadline. I also bring a strong Web-based knowledge of uploading and preparing artwork for online publications, as well as strong creativity and experience in the layout, pagination, and writing. I have an unquenchable thirst for learning and growing in all realms of journalism.

Education

1979-1980	American Business College	San Diego, California

Diploma in Accounting/Certificate in Data Processing/Computer

1996-1999	Arizona Western College	Yuma, Arizona

Journalism/Criminal Justice

I attended school both full-time and part-time. I currently have 68 credit hours toward my bachelor's degree in both journalism and criminal justice. My goal is to complete my bachelor's degree within the next four years.

Experience
November 2006-August 2007, Managing Editor, *Bonners Ferry Herald*

I returned to the *Bonners Ferry Herald* as managing editor in November 2006, and during my time in this position, I recreated and returned this newspaper back to a paper that covered and served its local community. My duties included interviewing and writing about topics including breaking news, human interest, cops and courts, government, education, etc. My responsibilities included editing, supervising one reporter and a freelance staff, and comanaging the entire office in day-to-day operations. My reputation for integrity and ethics based on my ability to present all news articles in a creative, factual, accurate, and fair/unbiased manner is unequaled. I earned the utmost trust with my sources, which ranged from local citizens to city, county, state, and federal entities. Part of that trust is due to my knowledge of the criminal justice system and my proven track record of maintaining the highest journalistic standards and ethics, including respecting off the record comments, particularly when said comments could cause physical harm or danger to someone. I met all deadlines ahead of schedule; I planned and created the layout of this weekly newspaper, as well as the layout, stories, etc., for all special publications we produced.

December 2003-November 2006, Coeditor, Woodbury Reports, Inc. & Managing Editor of RuralNorthwest.com

As the coeditor of the Woodbury Reports, Inc., publication, my responsibilities included editing all materials submitted by the educational consultants with this firm as well as all outside submissions from highly trained professionals from within the struggling teen industry. I was in charge of monthly newsletter layout and design, conducted interviews, and wrote professional articles regarding the private parent-choice industry of private schools and programs. I also acted as the managing editor of an online newspaper at, **www.ruralnorthwest.com**, which covered the five northern counties of Idaho. My duties in this position included, writing, editing, uploading said materials to the website, and managing the budget, advertising sales, and the personnel and freelance writing staff. I provided the training to all in-house writing staff and freelance writers for both publications.

October 2002-October 2003, Editor, *Priest River Times*

In October of 2002, my publisher promoted me to the position of managing editor of the *Priest River Times*. In this position, I maintained a high level of trust, integrity, honesty, and professionalism in all aspects of journalism while tackling the additional tasks required in my position. I grew immensely as a manager, editor, and journalist over that year, and my abilities continue to grow with each new challenge. While in Priest River, I was instrumental in making positive changes at this newspaper by not only increasing public awareness, but also delivering local news back to this community and illustrating a high level of ethics and dedication to the area I served. This was evident in the increase in circulation and public response to the new design and content my office offered the public. I was responsible for all content, layout, and running of the editorial department in this office. I worked closely with my reporter as both an editor and mentor to provide the support she needed as a new journalist. Between the two of us, we covered all events, news, and sports for our local area, which included Priest River, Priest Lake, Newport, Washington, Oldtown, Spirit Lake, Blanchard, and Laclede. I covered and learned about the topics important to the people of that area.

November 2000-October 2002, Journalist, *Bonners Ferry Herald* **(Hagadone Corp.)**

I developed a close working relationship with local government, business, law enforcement, state and federal officials, community members, and numerous other organizations. Over these two years, I built a reputation based on trust, integrity, honesty, and a deep commitment to my ethics as a journalist. Through the investigative process, I learned, understood, and reported on a variety of issues ranging from local murder cases to human interest and community events. My responsibilities included editorial, photography, design, and layout of all special sections created by the advertising department. I met all deadlines in a timely manner and maintained a strong loyalty to my paper and community.

August 2000-November 2000, Advertising, *Bonner County Daily Bee* **(Hagadone Corp.)**

I began my career with the Hagadone Corporation in the Sandpoint office selling a new idea for a business phone directory. I spent three months selling advertising into the new phone book, designing the covers and ads, and editing the final proof for printing. I sold more than $16,000 in advertising for this 50-page book that covered our two local counties. When the book went to print, the position in Bonners Ferry opened up and I went back to my career in journalism.

1999-2000   Student/Housewife, Arizona Western College

During this time, I continued my education part-time and focused on my family.

1998-1999   Office Manager, Jaguar Fast Freight

I was responsible for day-to-day operations of delivery terminal, dispatch, records, and reports for monthly labor to revenue statistics, customer relations, and support.

1997-1998	**Editor-in-Chief, Arizona Western College**

I edited stories written by journalism students for grammar, detail, and accuracy and helped students with the creative process during story construction and data entry of all stories for publication. I set up college computer for full layout of the school paper, which allowed everything to be manipulated on the screen and dramatically reduced the time required to prepare a hard copy for the printing company.

1996-1999	**Full/Part-time Student, Arizona Western College**

I averaged 15-21 credit hours per semester with a 3.5 GPA and maintained a 3.7 GPA while attending part-time.

1995-1998	**Community Spotlight Editor, *The Yuma Super Shopper***

In my first professional writing position, I had a weekly column where I interviewed and investigated community events and organizations. During this time, I also wrote and edited a yearly publication called the *River City Guide* for the same corporation. *The Shopper* is a weekly paper with a circulation of 60,000 in the summer and 120,000 during the winter months.

The presentation for a federal cover letter is very similar to the presentation for a private sector cover letter. They should both follow business letter format. They should introduce the applicant and the résumé and add to the overall appeal of the applicant to the hiring manager. The federal cover letter should be carefully crafted, but the expectations for a private sector cover letter should be no different. The main difference is that while cover letters are standard for all private sector jobs, the need for a cover letter will vary depending on the agency and position for federal jobs.

SUBSTANCE IS MUCH BETTER THAN FLASH

In order to make an informed decision, hiring managers need to know exactly how you are qualified for the open position. Creating a résumé that is visually appealing, but that breezes over your work history and educational background will not suffice. Although the résumé should be well organized, appearances are not everything. Before a résumé reaches the hiring manager, it is assessed to determine whether the applicant is qualified for the position. An applicant is assessed depending on the department and agency doing the hiring in two ways. One way is by having the human resources staff read the résumé and application packet first to weed out unqualified applicants. The human resources staff uses a set of keywords as a guide for assessing the résumés. This is why the use of keywords is so important.

The second option is to have the résumés first assessed by an automated program. This program will scan the résumé looking for specific keywords. If those words are found throughout the résumé, the application packet will be passed to the next level. If the keywords are not found in the ré-sumé, the résumé will be discarded as not qualified. This is why identifying and using keywords and phrases is essential to the résumé writing process. *Identifying keywords will be covered extensively in the next section.*

Focusing on numbers

When writing your résumé and cover letter, it is important to be as specific as possible. This will give the hiring manager a better vision of how much you have accomplished professionally and how much responsibility you have had in your previous positions. It will also allow you to present more information in few words. The following is a list of questions you should be thinking about when writing your résumé and cover letter:

- How many years of experience do you have?
- How many hours of training you have taken on a particular subject?
- How productive are you in a specific time period? (For example, how many words you type per minute, and how many articles can you produce per month, etc.)
- How much time have you saved your current employer through streamlining procedures?
- How many employees have you supervised, recruited, or trained?
- How many people have attended your presentations, conferences, or events?
- How many events have your organized or led?
- What is the circulation of your publications?

- How many organizations have adopted regulations, strategies, or training methods that you created?
- How many customers or clients do you deal with?
- How many managers do you support?
- How many stakeholders do you interact with?
- How many people use a product or system that you designed?
- How much money have you controlled or generated for your company?
- What is the monetary value of what you have personally contributed to your company?
- How many transactions do you deal with per week, month, or year?

Although the following work experience section of a résumé is brief, it provides specific details that focus on numbers. Notice that for each position, the candidate states how many consumers she was responsible for and how many staff she trained and supervised. She also provides insight to the emergency training she received in past situations based on the number of people she could mange during an emergency. She could take this a step further by giving an approximate number of the investigations she participated in or the hours she has spent training staff or participating in the human rights board. She also should provide more information regarding her current position, which is currently the least descriptive section.

Beth M. Hadley, B.S.

STREET * CITY, STATE* PHONE NUMBER * E-MAIL
SOCIAL SECURITY NUMBER* U.S. CITIZEN
POSITION APPLYING FOR

EDUCATION	**Bowling Green State University, Bowling Green, Ohio** *Bachelor Of Science:* Education *Focus Area*: Recreation And Tourism Cum Laude Graduate GPA: 3.53

EXPERIENCE	Koinonia Homes	Independence, Ohio	5/2010-pres.

Case Management Specialist
Oversee implementation of 50+ individual plans in a day-habilitation setting for consumers with developmental disabilities. Responsible for supervision of ten staff members.

Koinonia Homes   **Independence, Ohio**   5/2008-5/2010
Qualified Mental Retardation Professional
Oversaw and wrote individual plans for 15+ individuals with developmental disabilities. Responsible for emergency knowledge of 30+ individuals with developmental disabilities. Trained and supervised 10+ staff members, and participated in new employee orientation as a group leader. Carried out special investigations after abuse or neglect allegations. Participated on a human rights board and ensured the safe passing of medications.

Echoing Lake   **Lorain, Ohio**   9/2006-5/2008
Qualified Mental Retardation Professional
Oversaw and wrote individual plans for eight individuals with developmental disabilities. Responsible for emergency knowledge of 50+ individuals with developmental disabilities. Supervised 8 staff members. Organized scheduling and worked on-call.

KEYWORD AND KEY PHRASE SEARCH

Keywords and phrases are used in the job description to describe the core competencies and traits the human resources staff and hiring manager will be looking for when reviewing your application packet. Several agencies, such as the armed services, use computer systems to scan documents and identify the number of keywords. Only the résumés that contain five to eight of the pre-determined keywords will be passed to the next stage in the hiring process. Clearly, identifying and using keywords is essential to being hired by a federal agency. The following paragraphs were pulled from the major duties section of a job description found on the USAJOBS website. Each is followed by the list of keywords an applicant should have pulled from the paragraph to use in his or her résumé.

Job position: Registered Nurse, Assistant Chief of Sterile Processing and Decontamination SPD

In the supervisory role, this position participates in assessing the decontamination and high level disinfection and sterilization processes inside and outside of SPD. The incumbent participates in assessing the environment, analyzing trends, transmitting data, communicating ideas, developing and proposing policies, initiating programs and systems, and collaborating in the management of resources. The incumbent must demonstrate knowledge in areas of patient care practices, asepsis, disinfection/sterilization, adult education, communication, and program administration.

Keywords and phrases obtained from this paragraph:

1. Assessing processes
2. Assessing the environment
3. Analyzing trends
4. Transmitting data
5. Communicating ideas
6. Developing and proposing policies
7. Initiating programs and systems
8. Collaborating
9. Demonstrate knowledge

Job position: Child Development Program Technician

The primary purpose of this position is to lead child development program assistants at entry level through target levels and provide guidance in conducting daily activities with children, room arrangements and enhancements guidance techniques interaction with children, meal service, to ensure they provide appropriate developmental care and instruction in assigned area of responsibility in a child development program. Designs, implements, and reviews activity plans. Prepares and implements specialized programs for child with special needs, i.e., handicapped children with disciplinary problems or learning disabilities of gifted children. Observes and evaluates children's development level and maintains records of progress. Plans and conducts parent involvement activities and encourages parents to become involved. Inspects annex and its bathrooms, storage areas and outdoor areas for safety, health, or fire hazards and takes steps to resolve discrepancies.

Keywords and phrases obtained from the above paragraph:

1. Lead
2. Provide guidance
3. Enhancement guidance techniques
4. Provide developmental care

---

5. Provide instruction
6. Design
7. Prepare and implement specialized programs
8. Observes and evaluates
9. Plans and conducts
10. Encourages involvement
11. Inspects
12. Resolves discrepancies

As an applicant, you will not know which keywords or phrases the automated system or human resources staff is looking for specifically, so it is important to use as many of the keywords as you can throughout your résumé. In addition to the position-specific keywords and phrases, it is important to include the core competency keywords and phrases. The next section will outline how to find these keywords; however, it is important to understand what they are before you begin looking for them. Core competencies show that you have more to offer an agency than just your skills for the open position, and they demonstrate that you are a well-rounded applicant who has a lot to offer.

The following are some examples of core competencies:

1. Ability to accept creative criticism
2. Ability to work as part of a team
3. Takes initiative
4. Seeks out information
5. Manages self
6. Models commitment
7. Open to new ideas
8. Responsive to other's suggestions
9. Can build positive relationships
10. Trustworthy
11. Active listener
12. Keeps promises
13. Risk taker

14. Creative thinker

15. Ability to think outside the box

16. Pursues opportunities for continued learning

17. Remains calm in a crisis

18. Multitasker

19. Ability to motivate subordinates

20. Represents the mission of the agency

Finding the right words or phrases from mission statements, job descriptions, and industry language

All the keywords and phrases you will need for both the core competency and the position-specific skills will be found in the job description, in the agency mission statement, in the career description, on the agency's website, and in the classifications standards, located on the OPM website. It is important to read everything you can about the agency and the position. This is vital not just to writing your résumé, but for excelling in an interview if you are contacted for one. The following steps will help you identify the keywords and phrases to use in your résumé and cover letter:

1. Look up the job description, agency mission statement, and classification standards for the position.

2. Print each of the documents as you find them.

3. Read through each document meticulously. As you read, highlight all the keywords or phrases you find.

4. After you have highlighted all the keywords and phrases, take a blank sheet of paper and write all the keywords and phrases into a list format.

Having all the keywords and phrases in a list will make it easy to read and refer to as you write your cover letter and résumé. As you use keywords or phrases, cross them off on your list, so you can monitor how many you use.

How to incorporate keywords and phrases into your résumé

Incorporating keywords and phrases into your résumé is as important as finding them. One of the easiest ways to integrate them is to use the keywords as your verbs throughout your résumé. Keywords are active words, and using them will help you write a strong résumé. The following are two examples of incorporating keywords from the job description for the registered nurse provided earlier in this chapter.

Example One: "Analyzing trends" was a key phrase from the registered nurse job description. Let us say in your previous position you analyzed obesity trends in children. There are many ways you could write that in a résumé, but only one way you can write it using the keywords.

- **Wrong way:** Collected information from ten school districts throughout the state and examined the trends in childhood obesity

- **Right way:** Analyzed trends in childhood obesity by collecting information from ten different school districts in the state

The first example is not bad, and it would be perfectly acceptable for a private sector résumé. However, if your résumé is being scanned through a computer program, it is not being read for content and information. The computer will look for the phrase "analyze trends," and your résumé will either contain the phrase or it will not. You should follow up your statement with some specific information about the research you did, such as the variety of means you used to gather the information, the amount of time you dedicated to the program, the number of children involved, what the data was used for, or the positive effect your analysis had on the situation.

Example Two: "Initiating programs" was another keyword. In your previous program, you initiated a new program to educate children about healthy eating and encourage increased physical activity.

- **Wrong way:** Developed after-school program to educate children on healthy eating and provided an increased number of opportunities for the children to engage in physical activity.

- **Right way:** Initiated programs for children to learn about healthy eating habits and get involved in physical activity.

The second example could then be followed up with some positive information or statistics about the success of the program you initiated. You can also add the number of the children involved in your program and the amount of time you spent developing the program. It is important to use the correct tense of the verb throughout the résumé. Despite the fact the keyword is in the "-ing" format, if you are discussing a position you held in the past, you still need to use past tense verbs. Perfect grammar is still vitally important throughout the résumé and cover letter.

Where to find the words and phrases that will get you to the next level as a federal job candidate

All of the keywords, phrases, and information you will need to write the perfect résumé and cover letter can be found online. It will be located in the job description, the USAJOBS website, the OPM website, and the agency website. If you know someone in a similar federal position or even in the same agency as the position you are applying to, do not hesitate to contact him or her and ask for advice. That person might be able to provide you with some bit of information that will make the difference between you being hired or not. Take the time to explore these websites and gather as much information as you can before you start writing the résumé. Preparation is the key to success in this situation. Without taking the time to identify and use all possible keywords, your résumé will not even make it to the person in charge of making the decision. Your résumé could be discarded by an automated system, and you will be back at square one.

YOUR ACCOMPLISHMENTS AND ACCOLADES

Supplying information about your accomplishments is as important as every other section of the résumé, if not more so, and can make the difference in who is hired. If there are two candidates who are equally qualified and have similar experience, professional accomplishments could very well be the determining factor between them.

Accomplishments will demonstrate to the hiring manager that you are the most qualified and that you are dedicated to your career. Employees who are willing to go the extra mile to get the goal accomplished stand out to hiring managers. They are hard working, driven, and motivated to succeed in their careers. Employees who work for the paycheck and have no commitment to their employer are not the ones who get recognized for outstanding performance.

It is important to be specific when you write about your accomplishments. Explain the project or the problem you were trying to solve. Briefly explain the importance and size of the project. Detail your role in the project. Explain the steps you took to accomplish the goals of the task. Finally, explain the results. Use as many specific details as possible and provide measurable descriptions. In writing about accomplishments, it is important to emphasize the importance of your role in the process. Although being a team player is an important attribute, now is not the time to be humble. Without exaggerating, explain in detail everything you contributed to the success of the project.

THE GOVERNMENT LOVES A WINNING EMPLOYEE

Chapter 1 of this book discussed the "retirement tsunami" the federal government is experiencing. It is interesting to think about how many companies really lose the majority of their employees to retirement as opposed to leaving for a better or different position with another company. The fact that retirement is the government's biggest turnover factor is a testament to the benefits of working for the federal government. Once people get into a federal position, they do not want to leave. This is a contributing factor explaining why federal positions are so competitive. Potential federal employees recognize how amazing federal jobs are.

The federal government looks for people who are ready and willing to make a career commitment. All federal agencies look for applicants who are the strongest and most qualified. They look for those who have stood out among the crowd in their professional positions, their academics, and their personal lives. Personal achievements, such as being published in a non-work related capacity, are also looked at as a sign of an applicant's strength and commitment. Accomplishments are a testament to the applicant's core competencies, which are sometimes harder to prove than technical abilities.

Often, writing down accomplishments, work history, qualifications, and other relevant information can be difficult. It requires a lot of brainstorming and possibly the help of others. In addition to thinking of all these things, credentials need to be provided to verify many of them. The following is a brainstorming list of things to consider when evaluating what information is most important to be included in a federal résumé:

- Academic degrees
- Professional training
- Positive work evaluations
- Publications
- Websites you write for or contribute to
- Honors
- References in local media
- Military service record
- Computer skills
- Language skills
- Work projects or groups
- Work product
- Public speeches or presentations
- News clips

- Performance evaluations
- Voluntary training or work-related seminars
- Academic transcripts
- Copy of diplomas
- List of merit-based scholarships
- Internships or assistantships
- Volunteer work
- Extra-curricular activities

CASE STUDY: USING A MILITARY BACKGROUND TO GIVE YOU AN ADVANTAGE

Robert Parker
Air traffic controller
Federal Aviation Administration (FAA)

I was in the Navy for six years working as an air traffic controller. When I left the Air Force, I worked as an air traffic controller in the private sector for a year. Then, the FAA hired me, and I have been with the FAA since August 2006. Overall, working for the FAA has been beneficial for me and my family.

When you transition out of the military, you are able to take a class that provides information about how to look for a job, create a résumé, and figure out things like budgeting and controlling living expenses. This is where I got the information I needed to make my résumé. Working as an air traffic controller for the Air Force certainly gave me an edge when I applied to the FAA.

I recommend working for the federal government because, although my job is basically the same as it was when I worked in the private sector, the benefits, pay, and long-term options are better. I also recommend starting a career with the military. The training you can receive while in the military is invaluable once you leave the military and being former military can give you a clear advantage when applying for a position with the federal government.

WHAT YOU MUST INCLUDE

Whether you use a résumé builder or create the résumé on your own, there are specific sections that must be included in all résumés. The first is contact information. The second is work history, and the third is educational background. These three sections are essential for even the most basic résumé. Even if you decide not to use the USAJOBS résumé builder, providing the same sections as the résumé builder is a good idea. *Each of these sections and the specific information each must contain will be covered in detail in Chapter 6.*

The résumé should include basic information about the position being applied for, such as the announcement number, the position title, and the job's grade. All of this information can be found at the top of the job description. This will enable the human resources staff to know exactly what position you are applying for without sorting through all of your information. Agencies typically hire multiple positions at the same time, so you cannot assume the recipients of your résumé will know which job you are interested in.

EMPLOYERS WANT TO KNOW ABOUT YOUR PAST

Depending on the agency and position you are applying for, the hiring agency might want to go back as far as 14 years into your professional and personal history. Thankfully, this level of scrutiny is reserved for applicants being screened for high-security clearance. For most positions, seven to ten years is sufficient. The hiring manager will want to know who you worked for, what position you held, promotions, transfers, and terminations, among other facts. It is important to understand you will not be able to hide information from the agency to which you are applying. For example, if you were terminated from a position, it is better to present the information up front on your own terms, rather than let the human resources department contact your previous employer and find out their version of why you were fired. Although you cannot lie on an application or in your résumé, you can present the most positive form of the truth.

The same holds true for your educational background. If you started a degree program, but never graduated, you do not have to say you dropped out of college. You can write, for example, that you completed 20 hours of classes in the health and human services department of Bowling Green University. It is important to always put the most relevant information first. On a typical private-sector résumé, educational background information would be at the top of the résumé. However, if your experience and work history is more impressive than your educational background, you can write that section first.

WHAT TO LEAVE OUT

Omit detailed personal information, such as information about your marital status, family, and social life. However, you can talk about volunteer work or personal accomplishments. Instead of using the section titled "work history," you can use the title "relevant experience." This will allow you to include non-work history that is still relevant to the position to which you are applying. For example, the example used in the keywords section referred to "initiating programs" as a keyword. If you are the volunteer program coordinator for your child's scout troop, this experience could be considered relevant experience. In addition, it will speak to your commitment as a volunteer, which is a testament to your core competencies.

STYLE AND DESIGN

When using a résumé builder, the style and design of your finished résumé will be uniform and plain. The writing will be in block form according to the sections, and the sections will be listed simply one after another. You can use spacing to create depth to the appearance of your résumé, but you will do so at the sacrifice of available characters. Federal résumés should look traditional and formal. Although it is acceptable to present more graphic appeal in a private-sector résumé, it will not aid you in a federal résumé.

The following résumé was created with the USAJOBS résumé builder. The résumé belongs to a current federal employee who has maintained and updated her résumé regularly. Notice how the résumé is organized and formatted. Although the applicant decided what information was included, the résumé builder chose the format.

Susan Marie Giddings
1234 Boulevard St.
City, State ZIP
(123) 456-7890

Country of citizenship:	United States of America
Veterans' Preference:	No
Highest Grade:	GS-101-12, 07-2001-Present
Contact Current Employer:	Yes

AVAILABILITY		
	Job Type:	Permanent
	Work Schedule:	Full Time

DESIRED LOCATIONS	
	US-IL
	US-IN
	US-KY
	US-MD
	US-MI
	US-OH
	US-PA
	US-TN
	US-VA
	US-WV
	US-NJ
	US-DC

WORK EXPERIENCE	USP Lee, FBOP	7/2001 - Present
	Jonesville, Virginia US	
		Grade Level: GS-12
		Hours per week: 40

		Case Management Coordinator , 101
		As the CMC, I am responsible for the monitoring and quality control of all Case Management and Unit Management functions and the technical expect for all related policy. I review all correspondences for compliance with national policy and local philosophy as well as correctness in terms of grammar, punctuation, spelling, etc. I provide oversight for the following institution programs: Central Inmate Monitoring, Inmate Financial Responsibility, Victim and Witness, Inmate Performance Pay, and Release Preparation. I conduct Operational Reviews, prepare needed corrective actions, and monitor compliance. I am responsible for all Correctional Systems Department functions including: incoming and outgoing mail, inmate property, receiving and discharge of inmates, and records maintenance. I supervise 10 staff members including bargaining and non-bargaining staff and a mid-line supervisor. I draft and update local supplements and procedural memorandums relevant to Case Management and Inmate Systems. I draft a variety of correspondence including internal memorandums, inmate requests and grievance responses, tort claims, and correspondences to outside agencies and individuals. I manage three different cost centers. This includes preparing annual budget requests, purchasing research, regularly monitoring expenses, and preparing monthly reconciliation reports, credit card purchase forms, and request for purchase forms. I conduct formal training for both staff members and inmates including: Institution Familiarization, Annual Refresher Training, Basic Prisoner Transportation, Admission and Orientation, and Release Preparation. I oversee the OJT training, as well as conduct training directly, for case managers, correctional counselors, and unit secretaries. I chair the Release Preparation Program and Inmate Performance Pay committee meetings. I provide briefings to the warden and other executive staff whenever necessary. I address questions raised by inmates, line staff, other department heads, and the executive staff regarding issues relevant to Case Management, Unit Management, or Inmate Systems during mainline, Department Head meetings, and in other formal/informal settings. I serve as institution duty officer two to three times per year. As IDO, I make rounds throughout the institution; address concerns with inmate visitors; provide briefings to the administrative duty officer, other executive staff members, and the warden, and test locator center, command caller, and other emergency systems. I have received outstanding evaluations for the past seven consecutive years and received three QSIs ('04, '05, and '08) and four SSPs ('03, '06, '07, and '09). I have received several other cash and time off awards. (Contact Supervisor: Yes, Supervisor's Name: Roger Cosgro, Supervisor's Phone: 276-546-4102)

		USP LEE	**7/2001 - 9/2007**
		US	
			Hours per week: 8

		Affirmative Action Committee Coordinator!
		This is a collateral duty. I ensure all reports are prepared accurately and submitted timely to the appropriate level. These reports include: EEO MD-715 01, Disable Veterans Affirmative Action Plan, Federal Equal Opportunity Recruitment Plan, Affirmative Action Plan, and SEPM Quarterly and Recruitment After Action reports. I coordinate recruitment trips and committee programs, manage the cost center budget, and conduct institution tours. I provide information to the Executive Assistance for inclusion into the institution's strategic plan as well as the Warden's Performance Plan. (Contact Supervisor: Yes, Supervisor's Name: Tracey V. Brown, Associate Warden, Supervisor's Phone: 276-546-0150)

		FMC CARSWELL	**8/1994 - 7/2001**
		US	
			Grade Level: GS-12
			Hours per week: 40

	Case Manager , 101
	During my years as a case manager at FMC Carswell, my case load varied between 60 and 200 female offenders of varying security and custody levels. I managed case loads at the SCP, the Low Security unit, the Mental Health unit, and the Medical unit. I prepared written responses for the following: inmate request to staff member, Congressionals, judicial recommendations, administrative remedies, and outside agencies and individuals. I monitored the Inmate Financial Responsibility, Victim and Witness, and Central Inmate Monitoring programs. I prepared packets for halfway house and MINT placements, furloughs, VWP, CIM, relocation requests, parole, compassionate release, and treaty transfer. Through the unit team process, I reviewed inmates' needs and made appropriate program recommendations, monitored progress, and made adjustments as necessary. I prepared, participated in, and made appropriate recommendations for in-patient mental health treatment teams, unit discipline committee, and compassionate release committee. I had more than 1200 hours of acting unit manager experience. As acting unit manager, I assumed the following duties: chaired inmate program review/initial classification meetings and UDC; conducted rounds for mental health/medical in-patient and out-patient, general population, seclusion, special housing, and outside hospital; stood mainline; and reviewed all paperwork prepared by unit staff.

EDUCATION	Northcentral University
	Prescott, Arizona US
	Some College Coursework Completed - 1/2014
	3 Quarter Hours
	Major: Business Administration, Criminal Justice Specialization
	GPA: 4.0 out of 4.0
	Relevant Coursework, Licensures and Certifications: Currently enrolled in PhD program with expected completion in January 2014.

	American Correctional Association
	Alexandria, VA US
	Certification - 1/2008
	Major: Correctional Manager
	Relevant Coursework, Licensures and Certifications: Completed the Certified Correctional Managers examination during the 2008 American Correctional Association Winter Conference.

	Kennedy Western University

	Los Angeles, California US
	Doctorate - 2/2004
	36 Units
	Major: Public Administration
	GPA: 4.0 out of 4.0
	Relevant Coursework, Licensures and Certifications: This was a non-accredited, but licensed, distance learning program that required both proctored exams and a dissertation for matriculation. My dissertation examined the validity of the FBOP's custody classification system as applied to predicting misconduct of juvenile offenders. The dissertation was completed with the approval of the Bureau's Office of Research and Evaluation. The completed dissertation is on file with this office.

	University of South Carolina
	Columbia, South Carolina US
	Master's Degree - 5/1990
	36 Semester Hours
	Major: Correctional Administration
	GPA: 3.59 out of 4.0
	Relevant Coursework, Licensures and Certifications: For my thesis I studied the impact of the education obtained by offenders while in custody and recidivism rates.

	University of Cincinnati
	Cincinnati, Ohio US
	Bachelor's Degree - 12/1988
	108 Quarter Hours
	Major: Criminal Justice Corrections
	Minor: History
	GPA: 3.225 out of 4.00

JOB RELATED TRAINING	Intermediate Incident Command System for Expanding Incidents for Operational First Responders (ICS-300) (2009)
	Advanced ICS for Command and General Staff (ICS-400) (2009)
	FEMA Correspondences Courses: Effective Communication, Decision Making & Problem Solving, Leadership & Influence, and Principles of Emergency Management (2009)
	Defendant/Offender Workforce Development Conference (2009)
	American Correctional Association, Winter Conference (2008)
	FEMA Correspondence Courses: Special Events Contingency Planning for Public Safety Agencies and Role of the Emergency Operations Center in Community Preparedness, Response & Recovery (2008)
	FEMA Correspondence Courses: National Incident Management System; Introduction to the Incident Command System; ICS for Single Resources and Initial Action Incidents; National Response Plan, An Introduction; Introduction to Continuity of Operations; Emergency Manager: An Orientation to the Position, and COOP Awareness (2007)
	LEAD, Phase 1 (2006)
	Management Development For the Future (2005-2006)
	Updated APO, Cost Center Management, and 504 training (2005)
	Situational Leadership (2002)
	Management Development for a Diverse Workforce (2002)
	Core Skills, Credit Card Holder and APO training (2001)
	Winner's Edge (1998)
	Cost Center Management and Steven Covey's Seven Habits of Highly Effective People (1997)
	Unit Management Position Development Plan (1994)
	Introduction to Supervision (1993)
	Cross Development Courses: Correctional Services, Correctional Programs, Community Corrections, Program Review, Employee Development, Personnel Services, and Inmate Systems Management (1991-1997)

LANGUAGES	**Spanish**

	Spoken:	Novice
	Written:	Novice
	Read:	Novice

AFFILIATIONS	Daughters of the American Revolution	Member
	Children of the American Revolution	Senior Member
	Girl Scouts, U.S.A.	Leader
	American Correctional Association	Member/Certified Manager/Manuscript Reviewer
	Boy Scouts of America	Unit Commissioner and Committee Member/District Co
	St. Dominic's Catholic Church	Parishioner

ADDITIONAL INFORMATION	Approximately 1010 hours of acting experience for the USP Lee Executive Assistant.
	Approximately 725 hours of acting experience for the USP Lee Associate Warden (P)
	Approximately 80 hours of acting experience for the USP Lee Associate Warden (I&E)
	Supervisor of the Quarter, 1st Quarter, FY2008
	I received three QSIs, most recently in May 2008, for Outstanding evaluation ratings.
	I received four Sustained Superior Program Awards, most recently in May 2009, for Outstanding evaluation ratings.

KEEP IT SIMPLE AND TO THE POINT

There are a few points you should remember when sitting down to write your résumé. The following list of key points should be kept in mind while writing:

- Résumés that are too long, unorganized, hard to read, or boring to read will be quickly discarded.

- Dividing the résumé into sections makes it more visually appealing and easier to skim through.

- Avoid using long complicated sentences. All of your sentences should be short and concise.

- You should always use an active voice while writing your résumé and cover letter. This will make the résumé more interesting to read and your accomplishments sound stronger.

- Using a passive voice will make you sound boring and unaccomplished.

- Show your enthusiasm in your writing.

- Make sure the résumé is completely free of errors.

- Present your experience in an understandable way.

- Avoid using contractions in your résumé and cover letter.

CHAPTER 6

Crafting the Perfect Résumé

inally, we have reached the chapter this entire book has been leading up to so far. Actually writing the perfect résumé is covered later in this book because like all writing projects, writing a federal résumé is a process. You cannot expect a résumé to be perfect if you just sit down and scribble it down having done no research on the expectations of a federal hiring manager, the agency you are applying for, or the position you hope to fill.

By now, you should be fully aware of the vast number of positions available in the federal government. You are up to date on the benefits and difficulties of applying for a federal job and working for the federal government. You have spent some time exploring the OPM and USAJOBS websites, and you found some positions you are interested in. You printed out the job descriptions, and you read over them several times very carefully. You know exactly what the qualifications and major duties are for the position, and you know how to apply. Now, it is time to sit down and write your federal résumé.

FORMATTING YOUR RÉSUMÉ

You should use a traditional format when creating a résumé for a federal position. Everything should be well organized and visually aligned. The section headings, such as education, work history, and relevant experience, should be left aligned and bolded to draw the reader's attention. The information for each section should be left aligned down the center of the page. The significant dates related to the education and work history should be right aligned. Your contact information should be centered at the top of the page. Following this format will keep the résumé professional looking.

When formatting the résumé, keep these items in mind:

- Use wide and balanced margins.
- Use a standard font, such as Times New Roman or Arial, which is easy to read.
- Use bolding and italics to add emphasis to titles and headings.
- Use bullets to organize key facts.
- Use plenty of headings. They help to break up the information, so it is easier to read quickly.
- Do not start descriptions with the word "I." It is understood that you are the one who completed the task being described. For example, instead of writing "I supervised 30 employees," you can simply write "Supervised 30 employees."
- Throughout the résumé, make sure the verb tense is accurate and consistent.

The following résumé is an example of proper formatting and organization. It has wide margins, which makes the information easy to read quickly. The applicant uses line separators, bolded text, and italics to add emphasis and distinction to different areas for the résumé. There are bulleted points and plenty of breaks in the text. The writer also successfully uses active words and avoids using the word "I" throughout the résumé.

John Brown

45 Call Street Johnsonville, TX 45721
457-555-2467
Myemail@email.com

Social Security
U.S. citizen
position

Profile	I have spent many years in the field of social work and psychology. My emphasis has been in working with children. I have experience working with families one-on-one as well as counseling children individually. All of these experiences have strengthened my ability to work with families as a child protective services social worker. I have taught and consulted in the field of social work as an expert. I have also played in the Western Piedmont Symphony Orchestra for 17 years. I am now the personnel manager for the symphony. In August of 2007, I began a career as a freelance writer. I have since had a number of published books, audio tapes, and e-books.	
Education	Ph.D. Natural Health, Clayton College - with honors MS Natural Health, Clayton College - with high honors B.S. Psychology, Appalachian State University	May 2004 December 2001 December 1994
Career History	**Alexander County Department of Social Services, Taylorsville North Carolina** *Child Protective Services [Social worker}* • Investigated reports of neglect, abuse and dependency in Alexander County, North Carolina. • Networked with organizations such as law enforcement, day care providers, and schools about the signs of neglect and abuse and when to make a report. • Assisted families with connecting to services in the community that can help them in situations concerning domestic violence, poverty, and substance abuse.	January 2003 - August 2007
	Catawba County Department of Social Services, Hickory, North Carolina *Child Protective Services Unit [Social Worker/ Case manager]* • Worked with families that have been substantiated as being neglectful or abusive to their children.	December 2000 - January 2003

	• Worked one on one and as a family on parenting issues; connected family to community resources. • Developed a plan of care and safety with families. • Assessed safety of children.	
	Appalachian State University, Boone, North Carolina *Family Preservation* • Worked with children who were getting out of juvenile detention centers in an early release program. • Worked one on one with child and with the family an average of 20-30 hours a week for 4-6 weeks. • On call 24/7 for emergencies that arose with families I worked with • Connected families with resources in the community. • Prevention of children returning to juvenile court system • Certified by a national teaching family association as a teaching family professional; re-certified yearly as a requirement of employment	1997 - 2000
	Homecare Management *High Risk Intervention Worker* • One-on-one with children in a variety of community locations such as schools and homes • Referred by local mental health therapists to work with at risk children while implementing a plan of care to allow child to succeed in the community. • Worked with children in home and school to reduce at-risk status and teach new skills to child with modeling and redirection. • Granted the title by the state as a Qualified Mental Health Professional.	December 1994 January 2000
	Western Piedmont Symphony Orchestra • Flute and piccolo player; contracted musician for the regular season as well as the Western Piedmont Chamber Orchestra • Personnel manager; responsible for hiring personnel for concerts throughout the season as well as other jobs on a freelance basis outside the symphony	August 1991 - present

	Freelance Writer • Write books on small business and have published three books to date; two other books are expected to be published this year. • Wrote and narrated audio books; wrote an audio book for audiolearn.com. • Wrote a number of magazine articles for *Herb Companion*, *Winemaker*, and *Precognito*. • Work full time doing freelance jobs for clients through Elance.com.	August 2007-present

Formatting mistakes to avoid

- **The solid block of words:** Although it is acceptable to write job descriptions in paragraph form within a résumé, it is important that the final presentation does not look like a solid block of words. The hiring manager should be able to pull out important points and attributes while skimming the résumé. If the information is not presented in an organized and visually appealing way, it is more likely that it will not actually be read.

- **The endless list of job duties:** Avoid writing your job title followed by a seemingly endless list of all the things you did in that position with little or no explanation. Although short, concise sentences are important, it is still important to add detail so the hiring manager understands the scope of your position and level of responsibility.

- **Overuse of semicolons:** The semicolon should be used for short lists of elements within a particular job responsibility. They should not be used to string together a paragraph-size list of job responsibilities.

- **Not enough information:** If you do not have an extensive work history, elaborate on the work history you do have. Avoid introducing a former job and then not explaining what your responsibilities were or how you contributed to the company or organization.

- **Acronyms:** Avoid using acronyms in a job title or description without first providing the full name. A position might be very impressive, but if the hiring manager does not know what it is, it will not matter.

Sections to include

The résumé should always include contact information, educational background, work history, and relevant experience or special skills related to the position being applied for. Although additional facts and areas of information can be added, these sections are the essential ones that no federal résumé should be without. If you decide to write your own résumé as opposed to using an online résumé builder, consider using the sections in the USAJOBS résumé builder. Otherwise, the following is a list of suggested headers to include if you have information that would fit within the category:

- **Awards and achievements:** This can include awards and achievements earned academically, professionally, or through another means, such as volunteer work or community involvement.

- **Licenses and certificates:** This section should include any work-related training, as well as a list of licenses and certifications, including the year they were earned.

- **Public speaking experience:** This section can be used to describe your experience in public speaking, either through work or through other related experience.

- **Consulting experience:** If you have ever held a consulting position based on your personal expertise, you should include that in your résumé.

- **Publications:** List the name of the publications you have been featured in, as well as the dates you have been published and the names of the articles you have had published.

- **Professional associations:** List professional associations with which you are involved. This is particularly important if you have held a leadership position within the organization, which you should also state in your résumé.

- **Foreign languages:** Being fluent in multiple languages is an asset when trying to gain federal employment. List every language you can speak, as well as your level of fluency. For example, you should specify whether you can speak, understand, read, and write in the language. Even if you are not fluent in all four areas, this information can work in your favor.

- **Military experience:** Since veterans are given preferential consideration, it is very important for veterans to inform the hiring manager of their military experience.

- **Volunteer experience:** Volunteer experience can be as valuable as work experience. Detail a volunteer experience you have that can be, in any way related to the position for which you are applying.

- **Special projects:** This section allows you to detail any special projects you took on, either through work or as a volunteer. This can include fund-raising, grant writing, and event planning.

Sometimes more is better

As this book has already established, federal positions are highly competitive. For this reason, adding more information than you would on a private sector résumé might work to your advantage. Although you do not want to sound long-winded, it is important to provide the hiring manager with enough information to be confidant in your ability to exceed their expectations for the position. The following are some ways to add detail without being long-winded:

- **Be specific.** Explain exactly what you did and accomplished in your previous positions.

- **Use measurable terms.** This goes back to the idea of using numbers to be more specific. Letting the hiring manager know numeric details, such as the specific number of people you have directly supervised, will emphasize the size of your achievements.

- **Tailor the résumé to the vacancy.** Highlight the information that is most relevant to the position for which you are applying.

ORGANIZATION OF THIS CHAPTER

This chapter will provide detailed descriptions of each section that should be included in the résumé. It will also provide examples of information to include in each section, as well as how to present the information so that it is well organized and easy to read. Although the final résumé will be slightly different if you choose to use a résumé builder program, the content will still be the same, and the examples will still be relevant. The chapter is divided into sections corresponding to those you will need to include in your résumé. Each section is listed in the recommended order you put them in your résumé. The information presented in this chapter is based on feedback provided by federal hiring managers on what they look for when they review a résumé, as well as on information gathered from the OPM, USAJOBS, and Avue Central websites.

THE GOVERNMENT'S OBJECTIVES ARE YOUR OBJECTIVES

One of the stated benefits of working for the federal government is the employees' belief in the mission of the agency and the purpose of their position. The federal government wants employees who will be committed to the fulfillment of their intended goal. For this reason, it is important to fully understand the mission of the agency to which you are applying. When you address your objective in applying for the position, you should be able to quickly and easily refer back to the agency's mission statement. Being familiar with the mission statement and agreeing with the goals of the agency will not only help you in writing your résumé, but it will also aid you during an interview with the federal hiring manager.

An agency's mission or objective will be available on its website. The objective of the open position will be listed in the job description. Both the agency's objective and the position's objective are important for you to read and understand fully. If possible, refer to the agency's objective in your résumé. For example, if the agency's stated objective includes offering timely customer service, then you need to include immediate customer service in your past experience, if applicable.

PERSONAL INFORMATION/HEADER

There is certain information that federal résumés are required to contain. This information should be included at the top of the résumé with your personal contact information. All federal résumés should include:

- Job announcement number, title, and grade
- Name
- Address
- Phone number or numbers where you are most likely to be reached
- Country of citizenship
- Social security number
- Veteran's preference if you are a veteran

All of this information should be center-justified in the header of the résumé. Make your name slightly larger than the rest of the print. This will immediately draw attention to your name, which you want people to remember. Directly below the contact information, add a solid black line separating the header from the rest of the résumé. This will help the résumé appear more organized and visually appealing. If you are not using a résumé builder, you can use one of the many résumé templates provided through Microsoft Word. Of the many options, consider using one of the formal and more professional styles.

OBJECTIVE

Although objectives are not required, they can add to the résumé's overall appeal and can help fill in space if you are lacking in related experience and/or work history. The objective should be included directly under the header, which contains your personal and contact information. Typically, in a private sector résumé, the objective states what the applicant hopes to get out of the position. When writing your objective for a federal résumé, keep in mind that the hiring manager will be looking for how you can contribute to or benefit the agency. Therefore, the objective should be about what you hope to provide as a federal employee. The following are two examples of objectives that focus on what the applicant has to offer, opposed to what the applicant wants.

- **Objective:** To obtain a management position, which would allow me to use my eight years of supervisory experience to motivate others and promote efficiency.

- **Objective:** To obtain a position where my expertise in human resource management can provide the greatest benefits for the agency.

QUALIFICATIONS

Throughout your résumé, you should take every opportunity to emphasize your qualifications for the specific position for which you are applying. Qualifications should be made evident in your education, work history, and experience. You need to carefully incorporate the keywords and phrases you identified from the job description into your résumé. Your overall goal needs to be to make yourself an exact match to the description of the individual the agency is looking to hire. The use of keywords and phrases will get you past the human resources staff and will make the hiring manager want to meet you. You need to make the hiring manager want you to be a part of his or her team.

Qualifications might include paid and unpaid positions. This means you can include unpaid internships, volunteer work, or independent studies, as long as they are relevant and applicable. This can also include accomplishments, accolades, and special interests or related hobbies. You should also consider including information about special projects you were a part of either professionally or personally. This might include fund-raising projects, community improvement projects, or professional development activities.

The following résumé demonstrates a unique way a candidate can present information. The applicant separates her experience into writing experience and related experience. Above both of these sections, she highlights her specialties in an easy-to-read format. Separating your past experience into different sections also allows you to include information from a position you held several years earlier. Although work history is supposed to be listed in reverse chronological order, related experience can highlight only those positions that you feel are the most applicable to the position for which you are applying.

Barb Hanson

oooo Juniper Way
City, State ZIP
E-mail
Phone number
Social security number
U.S. Citizen
Position applying for

Specialties
- ✓ Award-winning writer
- ✓ Thorough researcher
- ✓ Team player
- ✓ Meets deadlines
- ✓ Generates imaginative ideas
- ✓ Communicates clearly

Writing Experience
Fountain Copy, Baltimore, Maryland
May 2004 - present

Owner

Freelance work includes pitching ideas, creating concepts, and writing, proofing and editing copy for direct mail, brochures, newspaper articles, and websites. Clients include JCPenney Direct, *The Wall Street Journal*, *The Washington Post*, and *The Baltimore Sun*, Wireless Wave Magazine, and USNews Ventures, among others.

America's Dream, Alexandria, Virginia

May 2000 - October 2002

Director, Correspondence, and Writing

Responsible for drafting, editing, and proofing correspondence for the President/ CEO and the Chairman of the Board.

Editorial Director

Responsible for creating, writing, editing, proofing, and disseminating marketing and communications materials.

American Association for the Advancement of Science, Washington, D.C.

August 1999 - February 2000

Communications Specialist

In charge of writing press releases and media notices, editing a 300-page source book for media use, and organizing the press room (for 700+ media representatives) for the annual meeting.

Related Experience

College of Southern Maryland, La Plata, Maryland

September 2003 - May 2005

Adjunct Faculty

Responsible for teaching speech communications and developmental reading classes. Created and wrote syllabi, lesson plans, and classroom activities.

WWBT-TV, Richmond, Virginia, **WAOW-TV**, Wausau, Wisconsin, and **WVIR-TV**, Charlottesville, Virginia

February 1994 - January 1999

Producer, Reporter and Anchor

Generated ideas, gathered leads, and wrote news stories. Developed *Faith and Family* segment for 54th market TV station. Wrote and produced newscasts, and anchored both news and weather segments.

Education

Virginia Commonwealth University, Richmond, Virginia

Graduated Magna Cum Laude, 1993

B.S. Degree Mass Communications

PREVIOUS JOB EXPERIENCE

Work history should be presented chronologically in reverse order covering the last ten years of employment and emphasizing the most recent and the most relevant. Although you want your descriptions of each position to be detailed, the greatest amount of detail should be provided for the most current position or the position that is the most relevant to the position for which you are applying. You can also skip over temporary periods of unemployment or underemployment that include periods of six months or less. For example, if you delivered pizzas for six months after graduating college, you do not need to detail your work experience there. If the hiring manager is interested in an employment gap, they will question you about it. However, if the employment gap is greater than six months, you should supply information regarding why there is a gap in your employment. For example, if you took a year off to care for an elderly parent, you can list that. Go on to detail the duties you had during that time. Try to detail things you accomplished or did during that period that could still be considered relevant to the position for which you are applying.

The following is a list of the most basic information you should include for any job you include in your résumé:

- Job title
- Month and year for when you started the job and when you left the job
- The employer's name and location, including city and state
- The number of hours worked per week if the position was less than full-time

If you held more than one position within the same company, only list the company name once, and use smaller headings to denote the different positions you held. Likewise, if you worked for a company for a long time in the same position, and your job responsibilities and experiences are extensive, break up the list by using subheadings. For example, you can organize a job description by grouping responsibilities into categories such as supervisory, administrative, and sales and training.

Position your past work experience before your education unless you are still a student or just graduated with little to no professional experience. The hiring manager will be more interested in your current responsibilities and skills than what school you graduated from years earlier. The education section is important, but if you have been out in the working world for a number of years already, your work experience will likely be more important.

PAST ACCOMPLISHMENTS

List your accomplishments in reverse chronological order as well, but only include the accomplishments that are relevant to the position for which you are applying. When writing about accomplishments, be as specific as possible and describe them in measurable terms. For example, do not just write you designed an after-school physical education program for grade school age kids. Instead, say that you designed and implemented a daily after-school program for more than 1,400 students at nine different schools that is being copied in three additional school districts that will affect the lives of more than 5,000 grade-school-aged children. A list of strong words to use throughout your résumé when describing yourself, your experience, and your accomplishments can be found at the end of this chapter.

The following is the past accomplishments section of a résumé. Notice how the awards are organized by date and the full name of the award is provided. Although descriptions of each award are not provided, it demonstrates the candidate's overall success and recognition. These awards, if relevant to the position being applied for, can also be expanded in the cover letter or interview.

Jeanette Farkas
Address * Phone number * E-mail
Social security number * U.S. Citizen
Position Applying for

Awards Received
- Cambridge Who's Who Among Professional and Executive Women — 2007/2008

- Honors Edition
- Madison Who's Who Among Executives and Professionals — 2007/2008
- Emerald's Who's Who for Executives and Professionals — 2007
- Biltmore Who's Who of Professional and Executive Women — 2007
- Princeton Premier Business Leaders and Professionals — 2007
- VFW District Teacher of the Year Award — 2002, 2005, 2007, & 2008
- Three Who Care (Jr. League) Semi-Finalist — 2007
- Middlebrook School-Related Employee of the Year — 2000 and 2004
- District School-Related Employee of the Year — 2000 and 2004
- Multiple Honoree of "Who's Who Among America's Teachers"
- "Atta Girl" Award from Florida Future Educator's of America

EDUCATION

This section of your résumé should cover every college or university you attended. The first one listed should be the most recent, and you should work your way back chronologically from there. For each college or university, you can include:

- The school's full name
- The specific college or department your program or degree was in
- The address of the school, including the city, state, and country
- The degree level
- Your graduation date
- Your major
- Any and all minors
- Your final grade point average (GPA)
- The total number of credits earned
- The system of credits and whether the school counted semester credits or quarter credits
- Any and all honors you received while attending
- Coursework relevant to the position you are applying for

CERTIFICATIONS

All the certifications you list should be in order of relevance to the position for which you are applying. It is important to avoid using professional jargon and acronyms in this section. If the hiring manager does not recognize the acronym, he or she will likely not pay attention to the certification. It is best to provide the proper name and the acronym. For example, if you are a certified ESL instructor, you should write out "English as a Second Language (ESL) instructor." This will allow you to use the acronym again later if need be. Each certification listed should include:

- The name of the certification
- The year it was obtained
- The school or agency it was obtained through, including contact information of the school for verification
- Any other pertinent information regarding the certification

PROFESSIONAL GROUPS AND ORGANIZATIONS

Professional groups and organizations are, once again, a testament to your commitment to your career. They can also provide you with solid work-related experience and leadership opportunities. Professional groups and organizations can also be positive opportunities for networking within your field. List the professional groups you belong to in order of relevance to the position for which you are applying. For each listing, you should include:

- The name of the organization
- The month and year you joined the organization
- Contact information for the organization and location of the local chapter
- Any position you hold in the organization, including the start and end dates of your time in the position and your major responsibilities

REFERENCES

Providing professional references in the résumé is optional. You will likely be asked for a specific list of references separate from the résumé. Either way, you should be prepared with a number people whom you have already asked to list as a reference. These people should know you in a professional setting. You should also have ready some personal references who are individuals unrelated to you. These can be people who know you through professional organizations, organizations you volunteer with, or simply unrelated people who have known you for a long time and are familiar with your life accomplishments. Every reference you supply, whether professional or personal, should have known you for at least one year. The longer the person has known you, the better. For each reference, you should have:

- His or her full name
- His or her contact information
- How long he or she has known you
- In what capacity he or she has known you

EXTRA ITEMS TO IMPRESS A FEDERAL HIRING MANAGER

Extra items might include certifications if you chose not to include a separate section for certifications. Although they are not required, they would aid you in the position. For example, if you are applying for a position in management, and you have been certified in peer mediation, this might be helpful to include in your résumé. Although it is not required for the position, it will make you more qualified because the hiring manager will know you have been trained to deal with issues between employees.

You might also include any publications in which you have been published as extra items. If you have been published in a trade-related publication, you should include this in your résumé. You should also mention whether you wrote or created any type of training manual or program that might not have been nationally published, but was used within your previous company or organization.

The following résumé is a prime example of adding extra items, which can make the difference between who gets an interview and who does not. The applicant's résumé is well organized and not too long. He was able to include a list of publications, as well as volunteer work, computer skills, and languages. Despite the fact that the applicant only knows a little Spanish, he included it in his résumé. Any knowledge of languages other than English is important information and should be included.

Dan Meyer
ADDRESS
CITY, STATE ZIP
HOME PHONE
CELL PHONE
E-MAIL

Social security number   U.S. Citizen

Position applying for

EDUCATION	**Charter Oak State College**	Graduated November 2006
	Bachelor's Degree	
	(Communications, Psychology, & Information Tech)	
	University of Phoenix	Graduated March 1994
	Associate of Arts	

WORK EXPERIENCE

10/07 - Present   **Deputy Chief, Resources Division**
Seventh CG District
Miami, Florida
Resource manager/coordinator for most operationally intense Coast Guard district w/10K+ active duty, reserve, auxiliary, and civilian personnel. Oversees current year operational budget planning and execution of $41M operating fund, $36M energy, and $14M facility maintenance funds. Planning officer for capital plan, district-wide reallocation, and resource requests. Initiates, reviews, and evaluates all infrastructure plane and shapes priorities for >$500M physical plant. Supervise five branches comprising resource division including: financial management, planning, technology/security, administration, and quality. Executive officer enlisted personnel.

07/06 - 09/07   **Comptroller/Business Analyst**
Coast Guard Headquarters
Washington, D.C.
Managed finance, procurement, budget execution, and reconciliation activities of $70M annual recurring budget for Coast Guard Directorates and Coast Guard, Finance Center. Coordinated

HQ funding/policy development for all CG financial enterprise systems, including Core Accounting System (CAS), Finance & Procurement Desktop (FPD). Managed $20M systems contracts, developed resource justification/budget req for systems support, and met agency and federal guidelines (OMB, DHS).

06/01 - 06/06 **Chief Financial Officer/Comptroller**
Air Station Clearwater
Clearwater, Florida
Responsible for planning, development, management, execution, reconciliation, and administration of $6.5M annual budget supporting 12 H60 & 6 C130 aircraft performing Air Station Clearwater & Operation Bahamas, Turks & Caicos (OPBAT) missions. Responsible for daily management, supervision, accountability of procurement, accounting, warehousing, aviation supply, and IRM branches. Managed and administered $6.7M general-purpose property program & $23M aviation supply inventory. Supervised and managed large Coast Guard dining facility.

06/01 - 06/06 **Web Architect & Special Projects Director**
CG Finance Center
Chesapeake, Virginia
Responsible for planning, development, management, and execution of all Web-development initiatives, Web-enabled financial data applications design, development, and deployment. Supervised staff of systems analysts and designers, and managed all special development projects.

VOLUNTEER EXPERIENCE

05/03 - 05/06 **ODYSSEY OF THE MIND**
Land O' Lakes High School
Land O' Lakes, Florida
Odyssey of the Mind is an international educational program that provides creative problem-solving opportunities for students from kindergarten through college. Kids apply their creativity to solve problems that range from building mechanical devices to presenting their own interpretation of literary classics.

PUBLISHED BOOKS

How to Use the Internet to Advertise, Promote, and Market Your Business or Website with Little or No Money

The Ultimate Guide to Search Engine Marketing: Pay Per Click Advertising Secrets Revealed

The Complete Guide to E-mail Marketing: How to Create Successful, Spam-free Campaigns to Reach Your Target Audience and Increase Sales

The Complete Guide to Google Advertising: Including Tips, Tricks, & Strategies to Create a Winning Advertising Plan

The Secret Power of Blogging: How to Promote and Market Your Business, Organization, or Cause With Free Blogs

Returning from the War on Terrorism: What Every Iraq, Afghanistan, and Military Veteran Needs to Know to Receive Your Maximum Benefits

The Complete Guide to Affiliate Marketing on the Web: How to Use and Profit from Affiliate Marketing Programs

COMPUTER	Advanced User/Web Developer/Systems Engineer: Windows 95/98, Windows 2000, Windows XP, Windows Vista, Windows 7 Microsoft Office 2007 and 2010, Microsoft FrontPage, Microsoft Expression Web, Paint Shop Pro X2
LANGUAGE SKILLS	Fluent in English, and speak a little Spanish.
REFERENCES	Available upon request

The following is a great example of a résumé for someone who has years of professional experience and is looking to make a career change. Clearly, the applicant has been with the same company for a number of years, so instead of grouping all of her work experience into one long section, she has divided her experience up by the positions she has held. This allows the hiring manager to see how she progressed within the company and gained responsibility as she progressed. This résumé is very well organized and easy to read. It is very detailed and provides specific examples and numbers to explain her level of responsibility. She also began the résumé with a "skill profile." This allows a hiring manager who is in a hurry to quickly assess her skills before deciding to read the entire résumé. One way the applicant could expand this résumé would be to add a section for accomplishments and accolades.

Ann Northwood

Address*City*State*ZIP*Phone number*E-mail
Social security number * U.S. citizen
Position applying for

SKILL PROFILE

A results-oriented professional with experience in training, project management, and software implementation. An effective communicator with all levels of management, cross-functional teams, and government agencies. Demonstrated ability to manage multiple projects and teams, while building collaborative relationships to achieve corporate goals under deadline pressure. Certified in secondary education English and speech.

PROFESSIONAL EXPERIENCE

Thomson-Reuters Publishing (Formerly *West Publishing and Banks-Baldwin Law Publishing*) (1991 - present)

- 18 years experience in multiple aspects of publishing and data processing
- Consistently receive exceeded or far exceeded end of year evaluations and consistently surpassed all goals and expectations.

Project Coordinator **(2009 - present)**

- Lead cross-site team of ten editors and software engineers in building 11 Administrative Code Regulations into current Web-based system with an annual project budget of 3.5 million.
- Create and implement cross-site testing and training plan.
- Lead all cross-site training for editors with wide variety of technical experience.
- Analyze data to create and write system requirements for each of the eleven jurisdictions.
- Work closely with software engineers conveying system requirements needed for publishing data and ensuring quality.
- Solely responsible for submitting all system change requests

Project Lead **(2007 - present)**

- Collaborate with software engineers and cross-site system experts to redesign mainframe editorial system into a Web-based environment, including writing sub specs, analyzing code requirements, evaluating prototypes, and extensive testing with an annual budget of 2.5 million.
- Submit 80 percent of all system quality trackers in three of the seven subprojects.
- Evaluate variations within each jurisdiction content, writing rules for system quality checks, proposing process and procedure changes, and writing system change request for software engineers.

- Prepare six Cleveland jurisdictions to transition to Web-based software system through a series of training meetings and sessions.

Cross-site System Support (2007 - present)
- Troubleshoot and address training issues cross-site for 26 jurisdictions in Web-based editorial system.
- Translate mainframe tasks and recommend process changes for all 26 jurisdictions.
- Evaluate system requirement change requests and prioritize with software engineers.
- Participate in Publishing Systems Improvement Team.

Site Lead Systems Trainer (2006 - present)
- Support Cleveland Codes Group — eight jurisdictional teams, 75 person office on all mainframe and Web-based system, including troubleshooting, creating, and maintaining training materials, conducting training classes ranging from 10 to 25 users, as well as one-on-one training.
- Recommend process improvement changes and create production documentation.

PRIOR
Project Lead (2005 - 2006)
- Prepared six Cleveland jurisdiction teams, including 40 editors and system processors, converting from VAX system to Mainframe Server Editorial system.
- Analyzed data, set up conversion tables, ensured all production deadline were not compromised.
- Trained users.
- Recommended process and procedure changes.

Lead Editor (2004 - 2006)
- Supervised 20-person product team.
- Coordinated Indiana Law processing, including scheduling and planning three separate Indiana publications
- Created and maintained internal procedures.
- Trained team members on all aspects of the product.
- Acted as a liaison with the state of Indiana and headquarters.

RELATED EXPERIENCE

- **Teacher's Aide**, St. Mary's of the Falls Parish School, Religion, 2008 – present (volunteer)
- **Instructor**, Bryant and Stratton Business Institute, Richmond Heights, Ohio (1991)

- **Student Teacher**, Brecksville-Broadview Heights High School, Broadview Heights, Ohio (Fall 1990)
- **English Tutor**, Kent State Development Center, Kent, Ohio (1989 – 1990)

EDUCATION AND PROFESSIONAL TRAINING

- Word, Excel, PowerPoint, Outlook, Windows XP, and Windows Vista Knowledgeable in XML Agile, and using Wikis
- Westlaw I and II Training, 1995
- Kent State University, Bachelor of Science in Education, 1990
- Cleveland State University, eight graduate credits toward a master's degree in literacy development/reading endorsement
- PBS Teacherline: Completed courses focusing on technology in the classroom

INCORPORATING STANDARD INDUSTRY LANGUAGE, WORDS, AND KEY PHRASES

Federal résumés and cover letters should be written as if you are talking to someone who knows nothing about the position or the field. Avoid using professional jargon, acronyms, or industry-specific titles. However, there are exceptions to this rule. For example, if an acronym or industry-specific term is used in the job description, you can reuse it in your résumé. You can refer to yourself as an RN instead of a registered nurse.

Often, people fall in the trap of using the same verb or phrase repeatedly, not using an active voice, or not promoting themselves enough in their résumé and cover letter. If you find yourself repeating the same word, get a thesaurus and look up alternative words to use. The following are some words you can incorporate when writing your résumé and cover letter.

Transitions to add information:

- Additionally
- Equally important
- Likewise
- Furthermore
- Finally
- In addition
- As well
- Lastly

- Therefore
- Consequently
- Accordingly

Verbs:

- Assemble
- Forge
- Formulate
- Create
- Spearhead
- Design
- Implement
- Accomplish
- Master
- Achieve
- Persuade
- Galvanize
- Lobby
- Inspire
- Administer
- Oversee
- Govern
- Supervise
- Exercise
- Utilize
- Deploy
- Manage
- Generate
- Publish

Modifiers/quantifiers:

- Unrivaled
- Foremost
- Unparalleled

- Prime
- Single
- Leading
- Greatest
- Completely
- Effectively
- Fully
- Thoroughly
- Particularly
- Significantly
- Especially
- Extremely

Adjectives:

- Outstanding
- Superb
- High quality
- Excellent
- First-ever
- State-of-the-art
- Innovative
- Deadline-driven
- High-energy
- Award-winning

Other power phrases:

- Created from scratch
- Single-handedly
- Played a pivotal role
- Precedent-setting
- On time and within budget

CHAPTER 7

Designing the Perfect Cover Letter

In the beginning of this book, we compared the résumé and cover letter to a sales pitch. Thinking back to this example, consider for a moment if you received a letter introducing a new lawn care company in your area. The letter was friendly, yet professional. It was well written, organized, and composed with perfect grammar and spelling. It was printed on quality white paper, and it included the person's name and full contact information. Now imagine that you receive a second letter from a new man in town who has decided to mow lawns for a living. His sales letter is on cheap paper, it was hand-written and then photocopied, and the grammar makes it look like a third-grade student wrote it. Even for something as simple as a lawn-mowing service, whom would you call?

Presenting yourself as a professional will impress people even if you are fresh out of college. You do not need to have years of experience to be distinguished. The cover letter is like the wrapping paper used at Christmas. Although the hiring manager is truly interested in the résumé, the cover letter will set the tone for the presentation. Even a great gift can be dimmed if it is presented in a paper shopping bag. Likewise, a small gift can seem much more personal when carefully wrapped in beautiful paper and ribbon. For applicants with little experience, the cover letter can be their opportunity to convince the hiring manager they are worth interviewing.

IMPROVING YOUR CHANCES OF BEING HIRED WITH THE PERFECT COVER LETTER

Although a cover letter is not always required when applying for a federal position, it can increase your chances of being hired when properly written. The cover letter should be written with the same level of attention to detail as the résumé, because it will also act as a demonstration of your written communication skills. A poorly written cover letter or a clearly generic cover letter can hurt your chances of the application packet even making it to the hiring manager. According to the career services department at Virginia Tech University, the cover letter should accomplish a number of things. It should:

1. Explain why you are sending a résumé.
2. Convince the reader to read your résumé.
3. Bring attention to specific details in your background that particularly qualify you for the position.
4. Refer to specific information that was requested in the application packet.
5. Reflect your overall attitude.

The language and tone used in your cover letter will also increase your chances of being hired. Although the cover letter should be professional, it should also be inviting and energetic. It is important to convey to the hiring manager that you are eager to work hard toward the agency's goals. It is important to remember that the hiring manager will be most interested in what you have to offer the agency and what makes you better than all the other applicants. Obviously, you will not know who else has applied for the position or how their résumés and cover letters compare to yours. Because of that, you need to present everything you have to offer. This is not the time to be modest or hold back. Assuming that you can highlight certain achievements during the interview might cause you to not get an interview. Demonstrate how your experience and background has prepared you for this exact position. Focus on what you can offer the hiring manager and how you will contribute to the agency.

The following cover letter is an ideal example. The introduction is engaging, as well as detailed. The body paragraph provides specific examples with a focus on numbers. The example uses an active voice, solid transitions, and several action words. The cover letter is easy to read and effectively translates the applicant's enthusiasm regarding the open position. The cover letter is also well organized and visually appealing. Her name is larger and darker than the rest of the font, which makes it stand out.

Ruth Adell Paine
123 Boulevard – City, State ZIP – 123-456-7890 – myemail@email.com

October 21, 2010

Dear Jonathan Franklin:

With documented success in forging strategic relationships to maximize revenue growth, I am writing in response to your search for a senior sales representative. Skilled in product knowledge, troubleshooting, competitive advantage, construction project management, customer needs, and logistics/procurement/delivery, I will be a valuable asset within your organization.

During my 15+ years of experience, I turned around an underperforming distribution center, enabling the branch to rank within the 15 top branches among 65 locations. In addition, I decreased inventory from $2.9M to $500K, increased revenue 300 percent in two years, and drove sales from $200K to $2M in five years. I am confident I will equally impact your company.

Moreover, I maintain in-depth product knowledge to boost overall customer satisfaction and deliver new, repeat, and referral business. Eager to detail my achievements and discuss your strategic plans, I look forward to your reply. Meanwhile, thank you for your attention.

Sincerely,
Ruth Adell Paine
Enclosure

Name-dropping

The cover letter is also an opportunity for you to mention someone in the agency you already have a connection with. Although name-dropping will not guarantee you a position, it can peak an interest in you. The hiring manager might go to the person you mentioned to ask about you and your qualifications. Some positions, such as Congressional aids, rely more heavily on name-dropping than other positions. However, you do need to be very careful and concise in how you incorporate an internal contact into your cover letter. The following two cover letters provide examples of effective and ineffective name-dropping.

The first cover letter is an effective approach to name-dropping. The applicant establishes a personal connection to the person, whom she says informed her about the open position. Then at the end of the letter, she refers back to her personal connection, and how it increases her qualifications for the position. In addition to effectively name-dropping, the applicant's cover letter is well organized, clear, concise, and specific.

The second cover letter is an ineffective attempt at name-dropping. The applicant refers to her knowledge of the agency through her uncle, but fails to mention her uncle's name. Without that detail, the introduction might well have been made up.

Sandy SMITH
123 Boulevard St. * City * State * ZIP* 123-456-7890* myemail@email.com

May 10, 2009

Helen Martinez
Chief of Staff
Congressman John Jones' Office

Dear Helen Martinez:

Sarah Richardson informed me that Congressman Jones is looking for a legislative assistant to work in the areas of education and health in his Washington, D.C., office. She suggested that I send you my résumé with her referral.

As you know, Ms. Richardson is one of the Congressman's greatest supporters. She and my mother grew up together in Florida's 7th District. My mother was thrilled when Congressman Jones ran for election, and I remember holding a sign with her on Election Day when I was seven.

Despite an early predisposition toward the Congressman, I came to admire him for my own reasons as I graduated from high school and attended State University. I am proud of his efforts to improve the local economy and serve as a strong voice for education. It would be an honor to work for Congressman Jones to help him fulfill his agenda in Washington.

Highlights from my attached résumé include:

- Graduation with a M.A. in Political Science in 2007 (holding a B.S. in Communication)

- An internship with an initiative campaign in Florida where I conducted research for press releases, collected and organized donations, prepared speech material for the grassroots representatives throughout the state, and fielded voter concerns as one of several people who answered the phones. The initiative was successfully passed in November 2008.

- A six-month internship with the American Heart Association in their lobbying department in Washington, D.C., where I met with a number of Capitol Hill figures

- Educational experience with work as an after-school tutor while obtaining my degrees

With ties to Congressman Jones' community and the necessary skills to serve in this position, I believe I am an ideal candidate. After you review my résumé, I am sure you will agree that I can make a positive contribution to the Congressman's office. Thank you for your consideration. I will follow up with you next week to schedule a time to meet.

Sincerely,

Sandy Smith

Landon Duttry
123 Boulevard St. City, State ZIP
123-456-7890   myemail@email.com

April 3, 2009

Tom Jones
Hiring Manager
Administration for Children and Families

Dear Tom Jones:

Your agency's reputation for producing the highest quality programs and delivering exceptional client services was known throughout my household growing up as my uncle worked for you for more than 20 years. Therefore, an opening for a program specialist was of particular interest to me, as I have long wanted to work for an agency as reputable in the as yours. As you review my attached résumé, please allow me to bring a few highlights to your attention:

- Five years experience designing road systems for the state development department, which was highlighted by the creation of the bypass around the Capitol, elevating some of the worst traffic jams (and accidents) in the state

- Seven years experience designing new plants for Big Corporation that made use of the newest technologies available at the time while maintaining strict safety protocols

- Graduated with honors from State University.

- Maintained a 3.7 GPA while working weekends for my father's construction business.

I believe my success has been a product of the exceptional work ethic I learned from my family. As your employee, I will make an immediate positive impact on your agency by putting that strong work ethic to work for you. I look forward to meeting with you to discuss these matters further.

Respectfully,

Landon Duttry

FINDING THE JOB POSTING
BEFORE YOU WRITE THE COVER LETTER

There are two primary reasons for why it is essential to carefully read the job description prior to writing the cover letter. The first reason is that many job descriptions will provide detailed information regarding the cover letter. The job description might indicate that cover letters are not needed. In the case of applications submitted through the USAJOBS website, cover letters can be submitted in the section for addition information or documents, which is where the KSAs used to be submitted. Unless the job description specifically states not to include a cover letter, you should include one. Even if including a cover letter is not requested in the job description, the hiring manager might assume applicants will know to include one.

The second reason is that some job descriptions will provide specific information they want to see addressed in the cover letter. Although a potential federal employer is no longer allowed to request that you complete short answer questions, he or she can request specific information in the cover letter. For example, a job description might request the applicant to provide information regarding abilities or experience in public speaking. In these situations, the cover letter is being used as part of the screening process to determine an applicant's eligibility. If the job description provides specific instructions regarding the cover letter, it is important to follow those instructions. Failure to follow instructions can lead to the application packet being discarded before the hiring manager even has a chance to review it. If the application packet is being mailed or faxed in and there are no specific instructions regarding what to put in the cover letter, then the cover letter can follow the format outlined in this chapter. Finally, if you are submitting your résumé as an attachment to e-mail, the cover letter should be attached to the e-mail, but also supplied in the body of the e-mail. This will allow the hiring manager to have a written copy of the cover letter after receiving your e-mail. Never send a blank e-mail with a cover letter and résumé attached.

LEARNING ABOUT THE GOVERNMENT ENTITY BEFORE YOU WRITE THE COVER LETTER

In the previous chapter, looking up the agency's mission and objective was strongly suggested. In addition to researching the mission, you should spend some time investigating the agency's website. Learn the organization of the agency, when it was established, and who the director is. You should also understand the goals of the agency, hot topics within the agency, and anything that might have caused the agency to recently be in the news. Knowing these things will allow you to sprinkle information throughout your cover letter and let the reader know you have done your research. Being prepared is a strong quality, and it will not go unnoticed by a hiring manager.

There are a variety of ways you can include agency information. For example, you can refer to the director by name and state that you admire the example the director has set for the agency. Then say that you wish to work under such great leadership. Although the sentence is still focused on you, it informs the hiring manager that you know for whom you want to work. Another way to include agency information is by acknowledging the agency's accomplishments. For example, after reading the Social Security Administration (SSA)'s Agency-wide Recovery Act Plan on their website, you learned that the agency successfully completed 317,000 retirement claims in 2009. You also know from reading the agency's website that they have been able to hire more than 2,000 new employees since the Recovery Act was put into action. You can incorporate this information into your cover letter — possibly in the follow way:

> First, I would like to congratulate the agency for the impressive number of retirement claims successfully completed in 2009. With the goal of more than tripling that number in 2010, you will need employees dedicated to prompt and distinct action.

Where to look for information on an agency

The first place you should go is the agency's website. Reading the website and being able to navigate it successfully is essential, and it should always be your first stop when considering a position. After reading the agency website, search the agency on a major newspaper website, such as *The Washington Post* (**www.washingtonpost.com**). If an agency has been in the news, it is likely to be covered in this publication. OPM also covers current news events that directly affect federal employees in their current news section. In addition to these websites, you should check the White House website (**www.whitehouse.gov**). The following is a list of online newspapers and websites that cover government news and might provide information about the agency in which you are interested:

- *Federal Times* (**www.federaltimes.com**)
- *Government Executive* (**www.govexec.com/**)
- *The Hill* (**http://thehill.com**)
- *Roll Call* (**www.rollcall.com**)
- *Federal Computer Week* (**http://fcw.com**)
- *Government Computer News* (**http://gcn.com**)
- FedSmith.com (**www.fedsmith.com**)

STYLE AND DESIGN

A federal cover letter should follow the format for a traditional business letter. For example, business letters are left aligned, the paragraphs are not indented, and there is an extra space between each paragraph. However, you can use bullets, numbered lists, or even a table to present your qualifications in an organized and easy-to-read format. Another area where you can step away from the formal business letter style is when providing your contact information. Traditional business letter format dictates that the sender's contact information should be right aligned at the top of the page. However, you can also chose to provide your contact information centered and in the same format as your résumé. In addition to possibly making your cover letter stand out among the others, it will also add coherence with the résumé. You want the cover letter to be eye-catching without being obnoxious. Do not use colored paper or colored ink. You should avoid pictures or images. Be creative within the realm of professionalism.

Syndi Seid, a leading expert on business protocol and etiquette, offers the following design and style tips for the cover letter. Her website (**www.advancedetiquette.com**) provides a wealth of information beneficial those entering the professional world. She recommends:

- Using standard 8.5 x 11 inch paper
- Using quality plain paper. Office supply stores often carry what they call résumé paper, which is a higher quality of paper than regular copy paper.
- Using consistent type size and style throughout the letter
- Keeping the margins balanced
- Typing the date the letter was mailed, not the date it was written
- Spelling out the month in the date
- Printing out the name of the state in the addresses within the letter, opposed to using the postal abbreviation
- Follow the contact's name with a colon instead of a comma in the greeting.
- Adding a two-line space between the greeting and the start of the letter content
- Ending the letter with a cordial phrase, such as "sincerely" followed by a comma

How to eliminate spelling and grammatical errors

It is essential that the cover letter is free of spelling and grammar errors. The cover letter, along with the résumé, will provide the human resources staff and the hiring manager with their first impression of you. A cover letter filled with errors will either communicate to them that you do not know how to effectively write or communicate through writing or that you did not take the time to proofread what you wrote. Either assumption will reflect very poorly on you as a job applicant. The importance of eradicating all spelling and grammatical errors was emphasized in previous chapters and when discussing the résumé. This point has been covered numerous times because of its significance. Have a strategy to ensure that every cover letter and résumé you submit is perfectly written. Consider doing the following to prevent mistakes:

- Use the spell check on Microsoft Word to check the cover letter for obvious mistakes and ensure that you use each word correctly. For example, spell check will see that the word "there" is spelled correctly even if you meant to say "their." You will need to spot these mistakes yourself. Do not rely solely on spell check.

- Print out the cover letter.

- Read the cover letter out loud.

- Have multiple people you can trust to provide honest feedback read the cover letter. This is not the time for hand-holding. Only ask people who can be honest with you even if the cover letter if riddled with errors, poorly worded, or boring.

Length

You should remember to include all essential information. However, you also do not want to appear long-winded and put too much information in the cover letter. You can refer to information in your résumé in the cover letter, but you should not restate the information in your résumé in the cover letter. The cover letter should be at least three paragraphs long and should not cover more than one typed page.

What to include

The cover letter should include your contact information, as well as contact information for the person or department the résumé and cover letter are being sent to. The cover letter should include an appropriate greeting and follow formal business letter language. The basic business letter should be composed of three to four paragraphs. The first paragraph will introduce to you and your résumé. The second and possibly third paragraphs will briefly state why you believe you are the best candidate for the position, and the final paragraph will wrap up the information in the letter and express your strong desire for the position. The cover letter should be signed and be accompanied by the résumé.

They want to know you are knowledgeable

Similarly to the résumé, the cover letter should be tailored to the specific position for which you are applying. The cover letter should demonstrate to the hiring manager that you are knowledgeable in the specific field in which you will be working. Although the cover letter should be brief, this is a good place to provide some personal statistics. For example, if you have been working in the field for an extended period, give the exact number of years. It sounds better to say you have been doing something for 18 years than to say you have been doing something for most of your adult life. Always be specific when providing information; specifics are far more important than creative writing. Another tip: If you have been published, give the exact number of times. Saying "I have been published eight times in three different national publications" sounds much better than "I have had several articles published."

What to leave out

Leave out personal stories. The hiring manager does not want to read about how spending the summer with your grandfather who worked for the post office when you were eight inspired you to want to work for the federal government. The cover letter is also not the place to tell the hiring manager about your struggles with binge drinking during your college years. Cover letters are not the proper forum for personal information. The cover letter is your sales pitch, which should include references to your education background, work history, and desire to exceed the hiring manager's expectations.

The cover letter is also not the correct forum to bring up any work restriction or salary expectations you might have. Many people have restrictions regarding overtime, travel, or family leave. Upon being offered a position, you will have plenty of time to discuss these issues. Similarly, you will know the salary range based on the job description. You will not need to know the exact salary and benefits unless you are being offered the position.

The following cover letter is an example of providing too much personal information. The multiple body paragraphs seem to ramble as the applicant talks about his move to New York with a friend and his subsequent failure to become successful. The loss of focus in this letter is unfortunate, because the first two paragraphs create a strong introduction. Overall, this cover letter is too personal, and the closing paragraph uses a passive voice. The applicant "hopes" they are interested, and he "hopes" he will get called for an interview. It is important to be assertive and use an active voice in your cover letter.

Zack Brown
Address
City, State ZIP
(123) 456-7890

April 2, 2009

Dear Pamela Jones:

Capturing the perfect smile of a beautiful baby: Nothing could be more rewarding than that — or more challenging. I, however, excel at capturing difficult images and would like to bring that talent to your staff if you will consider me for the photographer position you have available. I have attached my résumé and the requested samples of my work.

In my four years as a professional photographer, I have acquired a vast amount of experience and knowledge. This is due mostly to my time spent as a field assistant to Sam Waters, the well-known sports photographer for *The Washington Post*.

After leaving *The Washington Post*, I moved to New York with a friend, as we decided to live our dreams in the Big Apple. I realize I should be jaded by now, but perhaps because I grew up in a large metropolitan area, I was well prepared for what New York City would be like. I love the energy and vibe of this city. I currently work as a portrait photographer at Beautiful Smiles Studios.

I love my current position, but I read in your advertisement that you are looking for an applicant who can do scientific and technical photography, which is a field I have a particular interest in. With the training you provide and my natural talent at capturing the perfect shot, I will become one of your best photographers within months.

I am willing to start at the very basic level and will be more than happy to help set up for shoots on different locations or maintain the studio, and I would even enjoy learning more about the lab side of things in terms of developing the pictures.

Thank you very much for taking the time to read this letter. I hope that I have piqued your interest with my enthusiasm. After you have reviewed my enclosed submissions, I hope you will decide to schedule an interview with me. I look forward to hearing from you soon.

Sincerely,

Zack Brown

Do not include anything you would not like to see in a newspaper or on the Internet

Although not common, it is possible that information you include in your résumé and cover letter will become public information. This could be as simple as an article on the agency's website introducing new employees. Keep in mind that everything you write can be called into question. Use the cover letter as an opportunity to brag about yourself, but never embellish the truth. Do not add little quips or facts about yourself that you would not want everyone to know.

Do not get too personal or friendly

When applying for a position with the federal government, you are taking on the responsibility of representing the federal agency you will be working for. This representation is taken very seriously, and professionalism is expected at all times. Although some situations warrant a casual or even personal demeanor, the way in which you speak in your cover letter is not one of those situations. It has already been established that the format and the language of the cover letter should be professional; the content needs to be equally professional. Avoid using slang, family sayings, or family stories to make a point. Clichés are not appropriate in a cover letter.

ADOPTING THE GOVERNMENT'S MISSION

The mission statement of the agency you are applying for will contain the core values and goals of the agency. Essentially, it will contain the purpose for its existence. For example, the following is the mission statement of the U.S. Department of Transportation.

> "Serve the United States by ensuring a fast, safe, efficient, accessible, and convenient transportation system that meets our vital national interests and enhances the quality of life of the American people, today and into the future."

In your cover letter, it is important to incorporate the agency's mission into your personal goals and aspirations. The following is an example of how the agency's mission can be made a personal mission.

> I appreciate the mission of the U.S. Department of Transportation. As a dedicated employee of the Ohio State Department of Transportation for the past eight years, I have been committed to improving the quality of life for Ohioans by aiding in the safe and efficient access to our state's highway system.

The following cover letter is a great example of making the agency's mission a personal mission. The applicant goes so far as to quote the goal of the agency in her introduction. She uses specific examples in her body paragraphs, and her letter is concise and assertive. This is a very effective cover letter.

Michelle Artelle
Address Road – City, State ZIP
(123) 456-7890–myemail@email.com

November 5, 2008
Daniel Radcliff
Address
City, State ZIP

Dear Daniel Radcliff:

I am writing to express my interest in the senior manager of international training position with your agency. With more than 16 years of training, management, and leadership experience, I have the skills necessary to further your stated goal of "training individuals who can work independently to draw greater strength and productivity through cooperation and teamwork."

As a training specialist and program coordinator with the state of Iowa, I was responsible for developing and delivering training for 300+ staff members, determining the best training methodology, and leading a team of five trainers to successfully deliver quality training. As the training center manager for VITREX Corporation, I led a team of six trainers, helping them develop their skills in delivering quality training for authorized Microsoft and Novell training classes.

My self-initiative and desire to help others succeed will be a wonderful asset to your agency's training program. The attached résumé highlights my background and qualifications. I am thrilled about this opportunity and welcome the chance to provide specific examples of my ten years of training experience.

I would like to meet with you to further discuss how I can be an asset to your program. I look forward to hearing from you to schedule an interview at your earliest convenience. Thank you for your consideration.

Sincerely,

Michelle Artelle

Where to find an agency's mission

Every government agency has a mission statement, and their mission statement can be found on the agency's official website. Go to the agency's home page, and then click on the "About" tab, which is typically at the top of the home page. That button will direct you to another page with general information about the agency including the official mission statement.

THE BASICS: FORMATTING EACH SECTION OF THE COVER LETTER

The following sections will cover information regarding each section of the cover letter. The following is a basic example of what a traditional cover letter will look like when formatted:

> Your address
> City, State ZIP
> Today's date
>
> Name of Contact
> Contact Person's Title
> Name of Agency
> Address provided in job description
> City, State ZIP
> RE: name of position and job description number
>
> Dear [name of contact person]:
>
> Introduction
>
> Middle (This is where you can add bulleted points if desired.)
>
> Conclusion
>
> Sincerely,
>
> Signature
>
> Your full name
>
> Enclosures: Résumé

Knowing whom to address your cover letter to

The cover letter should be addressed to the person listed in the job description as the hiring manager or hiring staff. The greeting should also be professional. For example, if the job description says to send résumés to Ms. Gerry Harkins, this is how the letter should be addressed. Never address the letter to Gerry or Mrs. Gerry Harkins. Also, do not add "Ms. or Mr." to a name if you do not specifically know the person. Confusing the gender of a contact based on their name is a significant mistake. There are a wide variety of gender-neutral names, and you do not want to offend the person who receives your résumé. If you are only provided with the contact person's first and last name, only use this information. For example, if the contact is listed as "Sandy White," open the letter with "Dear Sandy White." Another option is to call the agency and ask whom the cover letter and résumé should be addressed to. You will likely speak with an administrative assistant, who can tell you how the contact should be addressed. Finally, always spell the contact's name correctly. If you receive the contact's name over the phone, confirm with the person you speak with how to spell it.

As long as you have the contact's name, the salutation for the letter should be "Dear." If you do not have the contact's name, you can open the letter with "Dear Hiring Manager" or "Greetings." Avoid phrases like, "To Whom it May Concern," which is impersonal and more appropriate for a letter of compliment or complaint to a company. Also, never use phrases that are gender-based, such as "Dear Sirs." Once again, you do not want to offend the person receiving your résumé.

Your contact information

Your contact information should be provided in the upper right-hand side of the page, and it should be right aligned. You might also choose to provide your contact information centered at the top of the page. It should include your name and address, which should be the same name and address provided at the top of the résumé. Although a phone number, cell number, or e-mail address are not needed on the cover letter because they are provided on the résumé, it does not hurt to add them. The following are three examples of how you might chose to present your contact information. Note that the third example takes up less room than the first two. This style is ideal for longer cover letters, because it gives you more space to write.

Example 1:

Melanie Williamson
1234 Boulevard Street
City, State ZIP
(123) 456-7890
July, 4, 2010

Example 2:

Melanie Williamson
1234 Boulevard Street
City, State ZIP
(123) 456-7890

July, 4, 2010

Example 3:

Melanie Williamson
123 Boulevard Street * City, State ZIP * (123) 456-7890

July 4, 2010

Introduction — beginning

You should introduce yourself in the first paragraph of the cover letter and include the title of the position for which you are applying. It also needs to entice your reader to continue reading. All good stories start with a narrative hook. The Fiction Writer's Mentor website (**www.fiction-writers-mentor.com**), which is an online resource dedicated to fiction writers, defines a narrative hook as, "the literary device whereby you hook the reader's attention and intrigue her enough so that she'll keep reading." Starting a cover letter by literally stating that you are interested in the position or that you have enclosed your résumé are not narrative hooks. They might actually have the opposite affect and cause the reader to skim the rest of the letter. The following are a few examples of ways you should *not* start your introduction:

- I am writing in regards to the open position listed on the USA-JOBS website.

- I have enclosed my résumé for the position of ...

- I am interested in working for your agency.

- I would like to be considered for the open position of...

There are a few effective ways to start out your introduction. You can begin by stating how impressed you are with the agency's recent accomplishments, or you can open with how perfectly qualified you are for the position. If you are not sure if your introduction is interesting enough, have other people read it. If they feel encouraged to read the entire letter, you accomplished your goal. The following are a few examples of narrative hooks within a cover letter:

- As a multi-skilled registered nurse, I offer over 15 years of diverse experience and training in all aspects of nursing and nurse management.

- Congratulations are in order for Director Sheppard on being awarded with a Certificate of Excellence in administration. I am eager to work within an agency that holds such high standards.

- I was highly impressed to hear the Social Security Administration effectively tripled the number of disability cases it was able to process this year. I am confident that my training and experience will contribute to the administration's goals for the coming year.

The following two cover letters show the difference between an engaging introduction and a boring introduction. The first cover letter is carefully crafted and combines recognition of the agency, as well as an explanation of how the candidate will benefit the agency. The second cover letter provides next to nothing in the introduction.

Angela Atkinson
Address
City, State ZIP
123-456-7890
myemail@email.com

March 7, 2009

Prudence Karp

Dear Prudence Karp:

It is twice as hard to attract a new customer as it is to retain a current one. Your agency not only understands that fact, but also demonstrates that maxim by its willingness to put customer satisfaction first. This is why I am excited to apply for the position of customer service representative within your agency. With more than five years of experience in customer satisfaction, I am a perfect match for your agency.

During my previous employment at a market research firm, I conducted phone surveys on consumer products. I was consistently commended by my superiors and those I spoke with on the phone for my friendly tone, my demeanor, and my ability to make a long, tedious process of a phone survey more enjoyable. Through the combination of skills I gained during my previous jobs, I developed the ability to interact with a wide variety of people. I assessed their needs and communicated with them in a pleasant and effective manner ensuring customer satisfaction.

As a recent master's graduate, I bring education and experience to this position that are detailed in my attached résumé. After you review it, I would appreciate meeting with you to further discuss the immediate positive impact I can make on your team. Thank you for your time and consideration.

Sincerely,

Angela Atkinson
Enclosure

Solly Trotto
123 Boulevard Street
City, State ZIP
123-456-7890

Feb. 27, 2009

Dear Hiring Manager:

In response to your advertisement for a librarian, I am attaching my résumé for your review.

With more than 12 years of experience, I meet your listed requirements in the following ways:

- ALA accreditation and a master's of library science from the University of South Florida

- Experience as a bibliographer, reference librarian, and special collections manager

- Experience with faculty liaison work particularly the process of putting books on reserve for professors' courses

- Experience working with graduate students in acquiring their needed materials for theses and dissertation writing

- Instructional experience with resources such as microfilm, digital collections, and the Internet

I believe you will find me an ideal candidate for this position, and I look forward to meeting with you to discuss how I can make a positive contribution to your team. I will contact your office next week to schedule an interview. Thank you for your consideration.

Respectfully,
Solly Trotto

Enclosure

Middle — explanation

The second paragraph should briefly detail why you are qualified for the position, and you can refer to your résumé in this section. You do not want to restate the information in your résumé. This paragraph should present your qualifications in the form of a sales pitch. Provide information that might not have fit comfortably in your résumé. For example, the cover letter might address how your years of volunteer work for the Boy Scouts of America have prepared you for the position.

If you hold veterans preference status or should be considered for noncompetitive appointment, this is where that information should be presented. The middle paragraph is also an ideal place to explain employment gaps. For example, if you took off time from working to raise children or care for a sick relative, these are reasonable explanations. Use a conversational tone and active verbs. Avoid professional jargon or bureaucratic words.

The following is an example of a possible middle paragraph that effectively explains an absence in the candidate's work history. Although it provides personal information, her approach is still professional and focuses on her ability to fulfill the available position.

> When we moved here I was pregnant with my oldest. Now that my youngest has started kindergarten, I am eager to return to the workforce. Although I focused on my family these last seven years and have not worked for pay, I kept up with developments in teaching and biology by reading literature and attending conferences hosted by the American Association of High School Science Instructors.

The following two cover letters belong to candidates with little to no professional work experience. Although writing a perfectly crafted résumé and cover letter for a recent graduate with little work history can be challenging, the importance is to emphasize what experience you do have. The first applicant managed to write a compelling and effective cover letter based on her work experience as a college student. The second applicant, however, glossed over her minimal experience and wrote a rather dull cover letter. Her cover letter lacks detail, uses an active voice, and displays a complete lack of enthusiasm.

Barb Lamont
123 Boulevard Street
City, State ZIP
(123) 456-7890
myemail@email.com

Dear Julian Webb:

As a recent college graduate with a B.S. in communication from the University of South Florida, my attached résumé should demonstrate to you that I am an ideal candidate for your copy editor opening. I received more than just an education in my time at USF; I received practical, hands-on experience that makes me competitive in today's difficult job market.

Any writer will tell you they have a passion for the written word. I want to show you more than my passion. I want to show you that I can do the job as well as my competitors who might have more professional experience than I do.

To meet that goal, allow me to highlight a few aspects of my academic and professional career:

- I wrote and edited for the campus newspaper. As a student reporter, I published in-depth investigative reports on the counseling that victims of date rape were receiving at our campus. The series of articles won national honors at the college newspaper convention last year.

- During the summer of 2008, I interned at the *Chicago Sun-Times*. I was one of a dozen interns selected to work in one of the busiest newsrooms in the country. I spent 12-hour days copy editing countless stories. At the end of my internship, my supervisor, Jack Brown, said my work was incredible, and he would gladly serve as a professional reference for me.

- I worked on the college's online newspaper for course credit last fall. In this course, I learned about page layout, Web design, and HTML coding. Other than writing original content, I also wrote all headlines and photo captions for the paper. It was an invaluable experience, as it made me confident I can handle online duties in the area of Internet news.

I would enjoy meeting with you to further discuss whether I am the right fit for your office. I look forward to hearing from you in the near future to schedule an interview.

Sincerely,
Barb Lamont
Enclosure

Kristen Lindsey
123 Boulevard Street
City, State ZIP
(123) 456-7890
myemail@email.com

July 10, 2009

Judy Morris
Head Nurse

Dear Judy Morris:

I am writing in response to your job posting on USAJOBS.gov for a nurse's aide. Please accept my enclosed résumé for consideration.

As a CPR-certified lifeguard and a LPN student at Memphis Community College, I have the formal training necessary for this position. Additionally, with two years of experience in retails sales, I have excellent customer service skills that can translate well to patient relations.

After you have reviewed my résumé, I hope to meet with you to discuss how I can be beneficial to your team. I look forward to hearing from you to schedule an interview at your earliest convenience.

Respectfully,

Kristen Lindsey
Enclosure

Conclusion — end

Your concluding paragraph should thank the hiring manager for taking the time to read your cover letter and résumé. This paragraph should also offer the hiring manager one final reminder that you are the best candidate for the position and express your excitement for meeting in person for an interview. This paragraph should not present any new information; it should sum up what has already been written. However, if you have a preference in how you are contacted, you can add that within this last paragraph. The following are some examples of effective closing paragraphs:

- Given my passion for nursing, I would make an excellent addition to your team. A personal interview will allow me to reiterate my passion and commitment and explain in more detail how I can contribute value and expertise to such a prominent and progressive organization as the U.S. Department of Veterans Affairs. Thank you for the careful consideration of my application packet.

- I am hard working, committed, and highly skilled, which makes me the ideal candidate for this position. I am happy to discuss my qualifications with you further, and I look forward to hearing from you. Thank you for your time and consideration.

Signature

Your signature should go at the bottom of the letter. Use blue or black pen and sign your full name. Although you want it to look authentic, it should also be readable. If you are submitting your cover letter online, you can sign it, and then scan it back onto your computer. You should type out your full name below where you plan to sign your cover letter. Below your typed name, type the word "Enclosure" so the human resources staff will know there is more information included with the letter.

SUBMITTING THE LETTER WITH THE APPLICATION PACKET

The cover letter should be submitted along with the rest of the application packet. It should be the first thing the human resources staff sees when they pull everything out of the envelope. The cover letter should also directly precede the résumé. All of the credentials should be included after the résumé. If the job description instructs you to fax the cover letter and résumé in, then you should follow the same order. If the application packet is sent online, the cover letter, résumé, and credentials should be uploaded as directed in the application.

CHAPTER 8

Important Issues and Items for Getting Hired by the Federal Government

I n earlier chapters, we compared the process of participating in a federal job search to that of a salesperson pursuing a customer. Once again, this comparison can be applied. After a successful salesperson meets with a potential customer, the meeting is followed up with a phone call, a thank-you note, or both. For a salesperson, not following up with the customer may mean losing a sale. Salespeople make follow-up phone calls to see if the potential customer thought of any questions after their meeting. If the meeting resulted in a sale, the salesperson will contact the buyer to make sure he or she is happy with the purchase. This encourages both repeat business and referrals. Follow-up sales letters are used to stay in contact with customers without being overbearing. They are also used to remind the customer of his or her interest in the given product and notify the customer of any upcoming sales.

Following up with the hiring agency after submitting your résumé and cover letter will keep your name fresh and recognizable to the hiring staff. They are more likely to remember your name if they spoke to you on the phone or received a personal letter from you. Following up an application and interview with thank-you letters will also emphasize to the hiring manager your enthusiasm for the position and give them insight to how you function. A follow-up letter will demonstrate your attention to detail, as well as your organizational skills.

FOLLOW UP ON YOUR APPLICATION

Typically, you would wait until after the job closed, and then contact the hiring agency to reiterate your interest and thank them for accepting your application. However, under President Obama's 2010 Memorandum on the federal hiring process, the USAJOBS website will provide applicants with the ability to track their application's status. According to the plan set forth by the Presidential Memorandum, this feature should be available beginning November 1, 2010. This will allow applicants to know if they are still in the running for the position, as their application goes through the various checks. This eliminates the need to follow up on your application status, along with waiting without real information.

You can still follow-up your application with a thank-you letter. Wait a week after you know your application has been a received, and send a letter to the same contact person you sent your application to or to the address you used on your cover letter if you submitted it over the Internet. The thank-you letter can be very short and direct. Simply, thank the person for his or her time and consideration and tell him or her you look forward to hearing more regarding the position. This will emphasize your interest in the position. Likewise, if you are called in for an interview, it is important to send a thank-you latter following the interview. This can be mailed the day after the interview is conducted. This thank-you note should be addressed to the hiring manager who conducted the interview. Once again, thank him or her for his or her time, and express your continued interest in the position.

How long to wait

Although you will be able to track your application's status online, you can still follow up with the agency. Wait at a week after the job closes, and then send either a letter or e-mail, depending on the contact information you were provided. Your correspondence should thank the hiring department or manager for accepting your application, and reiterate your interest in filling the position. You can also add in the letter that you wanted to make sure your completed application was received and to let the hiring manager know that if they have any questions, he or she can contact you directly.

Who to address your follow-up to

The follow-up correspondence should be addressed to the same person your application packet was addressed to. This might be a hiring manager or human resources personnel. If you were not provided with a contact name, you might chose to address the letter in the same manner you addressed your cover letter, or you can call the contact number provided and ask who is overseeing the hiring of that particular position. Although less formal than the cover letter, this is still a business correspondence and should be treated as one. Address the contact person professionally, and avoid being too casual in the letter.

How to create a follow-up e-mail or letter

Because a follow up letter is still a business correspondence, the format of the letter should be that of a business letter. Your contact information should be at the top of the letter, and the contact person's information should follow. The top of your follow-up letter should look the same as the top of your cover letter. Mimicking the same style and format will create cohesion between the correspondences. The follow-up letter should be no more than one page long, and it should not be a repeat of your résumé and cover letter.

The body of the follow-up letter should be approximately two paragraphs. The first paragraph should be the thank-you portion of the letter. Because showing your gratitude for the opportunity to apply for the position is the main reason for the correspondence, it should come first. The second paragraph of the letter should reiterate your interest and excitement in the open position, and emphasize your expectation for future contact. Before closing the letter, you should also reiterate your gratitude for the opportunity. Be sure to close the letter with your full name and signature.

The first sample letter is an example of a follow-up letter used to follow the submission of a résumé and cover letter. The second sample is an example of a follow-up letter used to follow a face-to-face interview.

Ann Northwood
Address*City*State*ZIP
Phone number
E-mail

Marie Starr
Address
City, State ZIP

Dear Marie Starr:

On Tuesday, September 7, 2010, I submitted my cover letter and résumé for the position of case manager specialist within your department. I wanted to take a moment to thank you for the opportunity to apply for a position on your team. I greatly look forward to the possibilities.

Thank you also for taking the time to review both my cover letter and résumé, as well as looking over my credentials. I appreciate you taking the time to give my application packet your fullest consideration.

In addition to my experience and qualifications, which are detailed in my application packet, I will also bring a high level of commitment and enthusiasm to the position. I am looking forward to meeting you personally to discuss both the position and how I can best serve the needs of the agency.

Sincerely,

Ann Northwood

Ann Northwood
Address*City*State*ZIP
Phone number
E-mail

Marie Starr
Address
City, State ZIP

Dear Marie Starr:

I am writing to thank you for the opportunity to meet with you and discuss my possible future within your agency. After being able to discuss the position further with you, I am confident that I can not only meet but also exceed your expectations. My experience combined with my strong work ethic and enthusiasm makes me the ideal candidate for this position.

I also wanted to extend to you an invitation to contact me further. If you have any other questions you wish to ask or would like to schedule a follow-up interview, you can contact me anytime on my personal cell phone (549) 555-8564. I look forward to hearing from you.

Thank you for your time and consideration.

Sincerely,

Ann Northwood

PREPARING FOR AN INTERVIEW

When you are called in for an interview, you should be well prepared for questions that might be asked and an opportunity to ask questions. Prior to the interview, reread your cover letter and résumé. You should also reread the job description and the information you collected about the agency while you were creating your résumé. You should also visit the agency's website to see whether any new information or recent events have occurred of which you should be aware. Be prepared with questions, should you be asked if you have any.

Chose what you are going to wear for the interview prior to the day of the interview. This will prevent you from frantically trying on several outfits the day of the interview. You should also leave early to get to the interview. This will allow time for most unexpected delays, such as construction or getting stuck behind a school bus. If there are no delays and you arrive well in advance of the interview time, you can spend that time organizing your thoughts and mentally preparing to walk into the interview.

Going to the interview

Getting called in for an interview means your cover letter and résumé were impressive enough that the hiring staff wanted the opportunity to meet you. The interview is your opportunity to make them want to hire you. You need to be professional, engaging, and enthusiastic. Dale Carnegie, a well-known writer and speaker, taught readers what he felt were the six most important ways to make people like you in his book, *How to Win Friends and Influence People*. Carnegie taught the following:

1. **Show a sincere interest in the other person.** Learning as much as you can about the agency offering the position and incorporating that knowledge into your cover letter, résumé, and interview will demonstrate your high level of interest.

2. **Smile.** When you are first introduced to the hiring staff, you should greet them with a smile and make eye contact. Looking at the floor while talking or maintaining a grim look will make you appear unsure of what you are saying.

3. **It is important to others to have their name remembered.** When the hiring staff introduces themselves, they will tell you their names. Immediately repeat their names back to them as you tell them your name. This will help you remember who they are. Later in the interview, if you are responding specifically to one person, address that person by name.

4. **Listen.** Demonstrate you are listening by making eye contact with the person talking, not interrupting, and answering the questions being asked.

5. **Focus on the interest of others.** Focus your interview answers on how your skills and abilities will most benefit the agency, opposed to how the agency can benefit you. Remember the words of President John F. Kennedy, "Ask not what your country can do for you; ask what you can do for your country."

6. **Show the other person they are important.** If you follow the first five steps, you will likely accomplish the sixth in the process. Remember the interviewers' names, smiling, being a good listener, and showing genuine interest in the agency and the position will convey your sincere feelings toward the people with whom you are speaking. Keep in mind that the people you speak to in an interview could potentially be your future co-workers.

CHAPTER 9

Other Opportunities for Using Your Federal Job Résumé and Cover Letter

The opportunities available for those interested in working for the federal government are not limited to the standard full- and part-time positions found on the USAJOBS website. There are a wide variety of opportunities, including contract positions, internships, fellowships, and number of options for students who are interested in working for the federal government after they finish their formal education. Student opportunities begin at the high school level, but they are still limited and competitive. Those truly motivated to work for the federal government should be sure not to limit their scope, but instead, consider the full range of possibilities.

WORKING AS A GOVERNMENT CONTRACTOR

A government contractor is someone who does not work directly for the federal government. Instead, he or she works as an independent contractor for the federal government. The federal government uses independent contractors for a variety of situations. In some cases, contractors are used to finish short-term projects. There are many contract positions for professionals who are not needed full time. For example, the Bureau of Prisons will hire psychologists on a contract basis to work part time in various facilities. This arrangement allows professionals to pursue other opportunities, such as publication, without being concerned with representing the federal government. The federal government benefits from the situation because it provides them with the flexibility to eliminate positions or let contractors go. The contractor will sign a contract with the details of exactly what he or she is expected to do, as well as the pay and benefits he or she will receive in exchange for completion of the job. In some cases, a contract is for a certain number of hours a week that the individual will work for the federal government. Companies or individuals looking to gain a government contract first must submit a Request for Proposal (RFP). An RFP provides the agency all the information needed to decide whether the company or individuals are what they are looking for. The RFP should include an overview of the business or the individual's personal experience, as well as business objectives and benefits of working with them. If, after reviewing the RFP, the agency hiring is interested, the company or individual will be able to submit a formal bid for the job. This will include the particulars of the arrangement the business or the individual is willing to offer, including price and timeline specifications.

Although contractor positions are partially based on the proposals and bids submitted for the job, the federal agencies still want only the most qualified individuals to fill their contractor positions. Having a perfectly prepared résumé and cover letter to submit along with your RFP will enable you to show the agency your extensive knowledge and experience. Government contracts are highly competitive, and similarly to applicants responding to a federal job description, independent contractors need to impress individuals who have not yet had the opportunity to meet them. The only way to accomplish this is through a carefully crafted résumé and cover letter, as well as a well-organized, comprehensive, and impressive RFP.

The perks and the more adverse aspects

Being a contracted employee of the federal government has its pros and cons. On the positive side, the federal government maintains its end of the contract in regards to pay and length of service. A contractor will not be taking the risk of not being paid. The contractor also benefits by still being allowed to seek other jobs with non-federal agencies. The cons of being a contract employee include the fact that independent contractors do not get all the benefits that federal employees receive. Independent contractors do not receive medical benefits or retirement. However, the work schedule might be negotiable, which provides flexibility that an individual might not get as a federal employee. Another potential adverse aspect is that independent contractors can be let go by refusing to resign when the contract expires. Federal employees, however, cannot be easily fired. Despite the downsides of being a federal contractor, successfully completing a federal contract provides an ample amount of experience and possible contacts for future contract opportunities. Having a perfectly prepared résumé and cover letter will enable you to have the best possible chance of catching an agency's interest and ensuring you a contract opportunity.

Working for a company that has a contract with the federal government

A wide variety of companies have work contracts with the government. However, the employees of these companies do not have contracts with the government. They are solely the employees of the contracted company. Their benefits will be dependent on what the company offers. The hiring process will also be dependent on the company doing the hiring. Applying and working for a company that has a government contract is really no different than working for a company that does not have a government contract, which means you will need to have a well-organized and impressive résumé when applying to work for a company with a government contract. Although the hiring process might not be as rigorous, a reliable position will still be competitive. One positive to working for a company with an ongoing arrangement is that the work will likely be consistent, which does provide job stability.

Presidential Memorandum
Interagency Task Force on Federal Contracting Opportunities
for Small Businesses
April 26, 2010

President Obama recognizes the role government contracts can play in the economic recovery of small businesses. With that information in mind, he has made the decision to increase contract opportunities for small businesses, which includes businesses owned by women, minorities, and economically disadvantaged individuals. One of the goals of this task force will be to ensure that at least 23 percent of government contracts are awarded to small businesses. This memorandum is being put into effect because in light of the Recovery Act, the government has failed to award a substantial number of contracts to small businesses.

The first part of this memorandum dictates the establishment of an Interagency Task Force on Federal Contracting Opportunities for Small Businesses. The objective of the task force will be to ensure the objectives of the memorandum are fulfilled. Within 120 days of the date of this memorandum, the task force will provide the president with suggested plans of action to remove barriers faced by small businesses, expand outreach strategies to reach small businesses, find ways to increase the opportunities for small businesses, and establish policies that will aid in the successful fulfillment of this memorandum.

Within 90 days of the date of this memorandum, the task force will develop a website that will show the progress being made in developing the contract opportunities for small businesses. Finally, the task force will do outreach to make contact with more small businesses and small business associations. Government contracts provide small businesses with a reliable source of business, which can make a significant difference in their overall business. If successful, this memorandum has the potential to spur a great deal of business at a local level.

TEMPORARY POSITIONS

There are agencies that need an increased number of employees during specific times of the year. For example, the U.S. Postal Service takes on temporary employees during the holiday season to deal with the increased flow of mail. The IRS also hires additional temporary employees during tax season to help process everyone's taxes. Temporary positions, similarly to summer employment, are easier to apply for and can lead to permanent employment. For example, the U.S. Postal Service requires a written test for most candidates. Temporary employees are not required to take the written exam. However, if the temporary term comes to an end, and the agency decides to offer temporary workers a permanent position, those employees will then be subject to the written test or other qualifications that were waived.

In addition to seasonal positions, there are other types of temporary positions, which are not dependent on the season. For example, Congressional offices might increase their staff during an election to help cover all the needs. The Census Bureau also hires additional temporary employees to work during the actual census, which is every ten years. Although still federal positions, these types of jobs are advertised and treated differently because of the large number of people needed and the short period of time they are needed. Having a well-crafted résumé and cover letter will demonstrate for the hiring manager that you will take the position seriously despite the fact it is only temporary. Temporary positions make a great addition to a well-crafted résumé and can help you in pursuing permanent federal employment.

CASE STUDY:
GAINING CONTACTS THROUGH
TEMPORARY EMPLOYMENT

Jennifer Jacovetti
Partnership assistant
U.S. Census Bureau

During the four months I worked for the Census Bureau, I helped promote the Census and distributed information material to the general public. I also entered information into our computer program, sent e-mails, and coordinated team meetings. Although I am familiar with the USAJOBS website, I learned about the temporary opening through job postings distributed by the Census Bureau. My former employer also made me aware of the open positions.

After making contact with the hiring staff, I was required to complete a short test in order to be approved for the position. Once I was approved, I underwent job-specific training. I did not use the USAJOBS résumé builder when applying for this position. However, I do highly recommend it. The USAJOBS website is very helpful for those seeking federal employment.

From the time I applied for the position until I was actually hired was approximately two months, and the actual job lasted for approximately four months. Although I knew the position was temporary when I applied, I appreciate the experience and possible contacts it provided me, which could help me gain future employment.

STUDENT OPPORTUNITIES

Student opportunities are organized under the Student Educational Employment Program (SEEP), which was established on December 16, 1994, under President Clinton. The program is open to any student accepted or enrolled at least part-time as a degree-seeking student in a academic, technical, or vocational program at an accredited high school, technical, vocational, two- or four-year college or university, graduate, or professional school. Prior to the establishment of SEEP, the federal government had a combination of four different programs, which provided opportunities for students. The current program is divided into two components: the Student Temporary Employment Program (STEP), and the Student Career Experience Program (SCEP).

The minimum age for federal employment is 16, which also applies to students applying for a position either through STEP or SCEP. There is no limit to the number of times a student can apply for a position within the program. As long as the candidate is an active student, he or she is qualified. Students who have earned or are earning a GED are also eligible, as are students who are homeschooled provided they follow an accredited or state-provided homeschool curriculum. Students whose parents work for the federal government are also eligible for employment, as long as the position they are applying for does not direct report to their parent. Although this program does not exclude non-citizens, the students must be in the country legally to be eligible.

Student Temporary Employment Program (STEP) & Student Career Experience Programs (SCEP)

This program provides work for students regardless of their major or academic pursuits. The work does not need to be directly related to what the student is studying. Positions under this program do not transition into permanent positions. However, if students in this program decide they do want to work for the federal government beyond school, they can transition to SCEP. After completing STEP, students will have a great amount of experience and on-the-job training, which can be used to create a perfect résumé. Although this program does not provide the opportunity for transition into the federal government, it will look very good to hiring managers reviewing a student's résumé and cover letter.

This program matches students with work positions related to their course of study and career goals. Students work for a federal agency while attending school. After successfully completing SCEP, students can transition into full-time federal positions. This program enables students who are sure they want to go into federal employment an advantage over others by providing both experience and employment.

These positions are highly competitive. Students will need to perfect their résumé and cover letter based on what is likely to be a limited work history. For students with limited work experience, it is important to incorporate volunteer work, extra-curricular activities, and hobbies in a way, which will increase their appeal to a hiring manager.

Jobs for students and recent graduates

Are you looking for an internship, a summer job, or a co-op program? Or are you looking for a quick way to jump-start your career after graduation? If so, the federal government can provide those opportunities.

Summer jobs and student jobs

Most agencies offer student jobs and internships as part of the Student Temporary Employment Program (STEP). Some student jobs, such as science and engineering co-ops at the National Aeronautics and Space Administration and internships at the National Institutes of Health, relate to students' career goals. Students often get school credit, as well as pay. Other jobs provide experience that is more general. To qualify for a student job, you need to attend a high school, college, or vocational school with at least a half-time schedule.

Students can find internships, co-ops, and other jobs by checking the online database at **www.studentjobs.gov**. This site is run by the U.S. Office of Personnel Management and the U.S. Department of Education. It lists many opportunities. Agencies are not required to post opportunities on the site, however.

You can also check with the career guidance office at your school or call agencies directly. If you are looking for a summer job, start your search in the fall; some agencies begin advertising positions in October, and jobs often fill quickly.

Recent graduates

The federal government also offers special programs for recent college graduates to help them advance their careers. Participants usually receive special training and assignments and yearly promotions. Most of these programs are specific to particular agencies. You can learn about them by attending career fairs, contacting agencies that interest you, and searching the USAJOBS database.

One career-building program, the Presidential Management Fellows Program, is available in several agencies. In this program, management fellows receive formal and informal on-the-job training and receive assignments designed to further their career goals. The fellowship lasts two years and is open to people with graduate degrees in any subject. Fellows usually start at the GS-9 level of pay. They are eligible for the GS-12 level at the end of the program. Fellows who already have relevant experience can start at higher pay levels.

Fellows must be nominated for the program by their college or university. Check with your career guidance office for application instructions. For more information, visit **www.pmi.opm.gov** or call (202) 606-1800.

INTERNSHIPS

The Federal Career Internship Program was put into place by executive order. According to President Clinton, the purpose of the program was to "attract exceptional men and women to the federal workforce who have diverse professional experiences, academic training, and competencies, and to prepare them for careers in analyzing and implementing public programs." The internships are offered through a variety of different agencies. Internships are two years long, but they can be extended at the discretion of the agency. These are paid internships, and interns are offered competitive civil service status if they successfully complete their two-year internship. Once the goals of the internship position have been establish by the agency and approved by OPM, the intern will undergo job-specific training. Internships are competitive, and a well-organized and visually appealing résumé is essential to demonstrate the candidate's interest and enthusiasm for the opportunity.

SUMMER EMPLOYMENT

Many agencies have temporary summer positions available for candidates looking to gain experience in federal positions. The position may not exceed 120 days in duration, and it must take place over traditional summer months in order for the summer employment exceptions to apply. The exceptions for summer employment include the exclusion of any written test requirements. Agencies are also permitted to non-competitively appoint a candidate who worked in the same position the previous summer. In situations where candidates are not being rehired, the agency must hire through competitive open recruitment. Agencies are strongly encouraged to post summer vacancies on the, USAJOBS website. Applying through USAJOBS will allow applicants to use the USAJOBS résumé builder to create their résumé.

VOLUNTEER SERVICE

There are volunteer opportunities available to candidates hoping to gain valuable experience, strengthen their résumés, and build a network of people who can act as mentors as they pursue federal employment opportunities. Volunteering is also a great way to hear about position openings, particularly in the political arena. Many Congressional aid positions are spread through word of mouth, and knowing someone is an important route. An easy way to get involved as a volunteer is to join a political campaign during election season. Politicians running for election are generally in need of a large number of volunteers to help them spread their name and mission to the voters. Volunteer service with a federal office or agency should always be included on a résumé for a federal position. Additionally, the volunteer contact person's name should also be included. Although individuals don't typically need to apply for volunteer opportunity, having a résumé already prepared and on hand will allow volunteers to possible be assigned a specific task in which they have experience. Volunteering is a great way to network and make contacts within the federal government; it also looks good on a federal résumé.

GRANTS, SCHOLARSHIPS, AND FELLOWSHIPS

There are a variety of different grants, scholarships, and fellowships available to interested applicants who fulfill the set requirements. Some of these programs can be found through the USAJOBS website. When conducting a job search, filter through student opportunities to search for fellowship or scholarship programs. Agencies that provide grants, scholarships, and fellowships will also provide information regarding them through the agency's website. Searching the websites for agencies you wish to work for will reveal any of these programs if they exist. Regardless of the agency or position, federal grants, scholarships, and fellowships are highly competitive. Having a perfectly crafted résumé and cover letter is as important for these opportunities as they are for employment opportunities.

CHAPTER 10

What to Do Once You are Hired by the Federal Government

Once you have successfully sold your experience, education, and motivation to the hiring manager, the real work begins. Working for the federal government is both rewarding and demanding. You are now a public servant, and you must keep the goals and objectives of your agency at the forefront of your mind at all times. Going above and beyond the expectations placed before you upon being hired will put you on the fast track to advancements and promotions. The federal government loves to promote from within. The opportunities available to an outstanding employee are almost limitless. However, in many cases the new opportunities are not going to come to you. You need to be vigilant, watching for new opportunities, and prepared when a new opportunity comes along.

ENJOY YOUR NEW STATUS

Being hired into a federal position is something of which you can be proud. After searching for a position you qualify for, crafting a perfect résumé and cover letter, being interviewed, and enduring background searches, you were chosen from the assortment of qualified candidates. You will now have the pleasure of enjoying the many benefits of working for the federal government, including the job security and generous retirement opportunity. These two benefits are particularly important in an unstable economy. As long as you put in your time, you will not be dependent on social security when you retire.

Along with enjoying your new status, you need to recognize your new level of commitment to public service. Making it through the background checks and investigations means you have made a conscience effort to stay out of trouble and avoid possible public scrutiny. It is important to maintain that while in federal employment and always conduct yourself in a public manner. Some people believe things you do in your personal life should not affect your professional life. However, when you become a public servant, your personal and professional lives are connected. With the rapid spread of information and images in the Internet, it is important to always keep in mind that what you do outside of work could affect you at work.

KEEPING YOUR RÉSUMÉ UPDATED

Although many private industry jobs allow employees to be promoted and move around within the company without reapplying, the federal government requires employees to apply for all jobs. This is why it is important to keep your résumé updated and ready in case a new opportunity presents itself. If you created your résumé through the USAJOBS résumé builder, then keeping it updated is simple. Your résumé will be saved within your online profile, so you can make changes whenever necessary. Anytime you are given a new responsibility within your position or attend job training, it is important to add this information to your résumé. If you decide to continue your education while working for the federal government, update your résumé at the end of each semester with the number of hours you have completed toward your degree. Updating your résumé as you go will ensure that you do not forget to include new information when applying for a promotion or transfer.

Being prepared when opportunity knocks

Having an updated résumé at all times will allow you to be ready the minute a new opportunity within the government presents itself. As it has already been explained, federal jobs can be very competitive, and this does not change once you are in a federal position. Although you might be given preference over a non-federal employee for a position, you will not automatically be given preference over another federal employee applying for the same position. Higher-level positions, which are only open to current federal employees, will draw a pool of applicants who are all highly trained and qualified.

OTHER INFORMATION AND CREDENTIALS TO BUILD ON

You might be offered the opportunity for additional or voluntary training once in a federal position. Take full advantage of these opportunities. It will increase your résumé's stature, as well as show your immediate bosses that you are eager and ready to learn. This will work in your favor when you decide to apply for another position or promotion. If possible, continue your education. This will enhance your résumé, as well as your possible pay grade. Furthering your education will also help you pursue a career after you retire from the federal government — especially if you want to go into teaching at a university level.

You might also be presented with the opportunity to work on various committees within your agency. Although volunteering for a committee will involve extra work for no additional pay, it is an opportunity that will provide you with valuable experience, as well as networking, and it looks good on your résumé. It will show future hiring managers that you are willing to go beyond your basic job description and be a part of the overall team. It will also support any claims you make about aligning your goals with the agency's goals.

ONCE IN THE GOVERNMENT, IT IS EASIER TO MOVE TO ANOTHER POSITION

Although internal openings still require an application, moving around within the government is far easier than trying to get into the federal government initially. In addition to promotions, federal employees can also pursue lateral moves if they want to go to a different facility, geographic area, or simply try something new. For example, if you are working in a Texas federal prison and decide you do not like the heat anymore, you can apply for a position in a prison up north. You will maintain your pay grade, as well as your years of service. Moving to a different area, facility, or agency does not take away from your years of service with the federal government. Although attempting to make frequent lateral moves will not look good for you in the long run, there is no expected time limit that an employee should stay in a particular position.

CONCLUSION

Many of the positions the federal government has to offer are recession proof, which makes them increasingly desirable in a slow economy. Alternatively, a slow economy actually increases the need for federal workers in several agencies. The federal government gives hiring preference to displaced federal employees, which provides added security to employees who are in a position to possibly lose their job. In addition to this, the Recovery Act has increased the number of available jobs in the federal government. This allows the government to continue hiring despite the slump in private industry. Many agencies, including the Social Security Administration and the Department of Homeland Security have increased their pool of employees, as well as their efforts with money received through the Recovery Act.

WHAT TO KEEP FOR YOUR FUTURE RECORDS

Always keep an updated copy of your résumé on hand. The USAJOBS website allows you to maintain a saved copy of up to five résumés. Take advantage of this opportunity in order to be prepared when a better opportunity presents itself. Keep copies of your cover letter, as well. Looking back at the cover letter that helped you get hired in the first place might help you in the future when you are trying to write another cover letter. Keep all your credentials and certifications together and organized. Add any new awards or certifications you receive after becoming a federal employee to your résumé.

REWARDS OF BEING A FORMER FEDERAL GOVERNMENT EMPLOYEE

The benefits of working for the federal government do not end when you retire or decide to leave your position. Retiring from the federal government means you will enjoy a generous retirement package, which will prevent you from having to live off social security. Being able to retire at a younger age will allow you to seek other career opportunities while still receiving your government retirement. Many retired federal employees go into consulting work or pursue teaching opportunities. Being able to create a résumé filled with government experience will impress future employers or clients and boost your reputation and credibility.

Sample Federal Job Résumé

Daniel Green
myemail@emailserver.com

Objective

Looking for an opportunity to use my extensive knowledge and experience as a professional writer in a way that will benefit the Department of Homeland Security.

Notes

- Can type 80 words per minute
- Have spent the past half-year working as a professional writer through Guru.com, attaining dozens of clients, writing several books, and more than 1,000 articles
- Trained in various computer environments
- A team player that will work hard to achieve results
- Have published two stories in two e-zines
- Have written blogs, articles, e-books, paper books, and more

Work Experience

WillWrite4You Services   November 2007 to present
Owner
Responsibilities include:

- Writing blogs for:

  o Two blogs per week for **www.saharasoultravel.com** on Morocco Travel
  o Three articles per week for the post-secondary site **www.welcome2college.com**
  o Two blogs per week on Home Theatre
  o Two blogs and eight articles per week on improving your credit for OurCreditFix.com
  o Three blogs per week on crafts for kids
  o Three blogs per week for Integard (raceriver.com)
  o Three blogs per week for American Floral Distributors
  o Two blogs per week regarding wealth management

- Writing e-books on the following:

  o Ghost wrote a 35-page book on company outsourcing; completed this project in one week for a client.
  o Wrote an book on investing in index funds book for Hotspot Publishing.
  o Ghost wrote a 51-page book on microloans for a client; completed in one week.
  o Ghost wrote a book on court security measures; book totaled more than 100 typed pages for a client.
  o Edited manuscript on selling your house for a client; involved going over a 100-page manuscript and rewriting much of it.
  o Currently editing and rewriting a manuscript on druids.

- Writing press releases for:

  o **www.finalmotive.com**
  o **www.pixabit.com**
  o **www.experiencediamonds.com**
  o **www.birthdaysupplydepot.com**
  o **www.heatingoil4less.com**
  o **www.makingcashwithwebsites.com**

- Writing SEO articles on:

  o 100 articles on gifts for a client
  o 10 articles on commercial loan lending
  o 165 articles regarding meditation and mindfulness
  o 42 landing pages for www.techstore.ie
  o 20 articles on scuba diving and anniversary gifts
  o 20 articles on gazebos and jewelry
  o 30 articles on water pollution
  o 30 articles on turtles
  o Writing 20+ articles on children's birthday party themes
  o 30 articles on reverse phone number searching
  o 5 articles on corporate employee relocation strategies
  o 14 articles on tourism in Turkey
  o 44 SEO articles on various topics
  o 30 articles on water fountains
  o 40 articles on companies in Brazil
  o 10 articles on dating
  o 5 articles on night club management
  o Several articles on wedding flowers
  o Articles on tourism in Morocco
  o Articles on Chernobyl, dentistry, eco-cars, and much more

Purple Press   October 2006 - November 2007
Denver, Colorado
Editor
Responsibilities included:

- Used Adobe InDesign, I designed the 28-page paper each week. We were in competition with a daily paper, so the effort to be new and inventive was constant.
- Edited photos using Photoshop and Adobe Bridge.
- Wrote the bulk of the 28-page paper each week, handling interviews, writing, freelancers, and columnists.
- Edited entire paper each week.
- Handed features and the planning of future articles.
- Covered all the news and sporting events in the area, which includes six towns and cities.
- Wrote two to three articles per week for the Kootenay Western Star.

Gladiator Press   July 2006 to October 2006
North Battleford, Colorado
Sports Editor
Responsibilities Included:

- Wrote the sports pages (seven in total) for the biweekly paper.
- Laid out sport pages.
- Edited sport pages.
- Covered sporting events.

Rivertwist Daily   July 2005 to July 2006
Edmonton, Colorado
Reporter
Responsibilities Included:

- Wrote articles about community events in the area.
- Photographed community events.
- Wrote a business column for the paper.

Volunteering & Clubs

April 1998 - September 1998   Umpire in Chief of Spruce Grove and Stony Plain

- Responsible for scheduling umpires, sending out of paychecks, and speaking with irate fans.

April 2004 - April 2005   Member of Spruce Grove Public Library Board

- Working on the board assessing a variety of library issues ranging from fines to a new location
- Received a Certificate of Recognition from the City of Spruce Grove for my work.

January 2005 - April 2005   Chairperson of the Technology Committee for Board

- Assessing technology related issues and problems for the public library

May 2004 - October 2005   Member of Toast Masters Sundowners Club

- Writing and giving speeches, evaluations, and other club tasks
- Achieved Designation of Competent Toastmaster after writing and performing 10 speeches.

August 2007 - present   Director of Columbia Phoenix Players

- Handling the advertising and promotion of the local theatre company

April 2007 - present   Director of Natural Control Alternatives

- Volunteering to assist the environmental group's decision to oppose the City of Trail's decision to poison ground squirrels
- Handling press and promotion of group

Education

DeVry Institute of Technology   October 1998 - October 2001
Denver, Colorado

- Earned a bachelor's of science degree in computer information systems.

Hobbies

- Reading
- Writing
- Software design
- Hiking
- Camping
- Genealogy

Henry Aaron Crumpton III

Street Address   **E-mail address**
City, State ZIP   **(000) 000-0000**

CAREER OBJECTIVE

To work for the Defense Intelligence Agency in a research or media-related capacity

PROFESSIONAL EXPERIENCE

Dolphin Publishing Company — Sarasota, Florida   **December 2007 - present**

<u>Freelance proofreader</u>

- Read and edit manuscripts using Microsoft Word's track changes tool.

United Sports Foundation — Albany, NY
June 2007 - December 2007

<u>Public relations — intern</u>

- Assisted in scheduling media interviews with senior staff, foundation president, and professional athletes.
- Created and distribute press releases and handled incoming media requests.

- Maintained and updated database that included members of the media, professional athletes, and national governing bodies.
- Organized and filed media articles into the database.
- Sustained internal media tracking database and generated media contact lists (local and national).
- Wrote athlete bios, including Sportswoman of the Year for the 28th Annual Salute to Professionals in Sports Awards Dinner.

New York Islanders (NHL)/New York Dragons (AFL) — Uniondale, New York
Spring 2004

Media/public relations — intern

- Researched and located approximately 100 newspaper articles revolving around each team using major New York newspapers.
- Compiled, distributed, and analyzed articles for department heads.
- Assembled and maintained archive books of the articles for future referencing.
- Hosted and maintained the Nassau Memorial Coliseum Press Box on game days, communicating with extensive media personnel for Islanders games and Dragons games.
- Distributed statistics, game notes, and article packets for specific media
- Provided continuous ten-minute updates to specific media on the other NHL games.
- Circulated final statistics to NHL-New York, NHL-Toronto, and both teams' next opponents.
- Accumulated statistical analyst of each player throughout the season.

New Level Sports — Miami, Florida
Fall 2001

Research/communications department — apprentice

- Assisted in expanding the firm's client base through Internet researching.
- Updated and monitored players' statistics and performances daily throughout their senior years resulting in New Level Sports signing more than 95 percent of the players recruited
- Reviewed and updated daily the firm's list of recruiting contacts with Microsoft Access.
- Organized approximately 50 player profiles, including game statistics and letters of recommendation.
- Faxed and e-mailed profiles to coaches in the NBA, WNBA, and more than 64 of the top European Leagues who were seeking to fill positional vacancies.

EDUCATION

B.A. sport management, Flagler College, St. Augustine, Florida — 2004

CERTIFICATES

Principles of Becoming a Freelance Writer
Penn Foster Career School (Distance Education Programs)
Started: 6/2005
Finished: 10/2006

VOLUNTEER

Student committee leader/volunteer
2000 - 2001 fall Special Olympics and 2001 - 2002 spring/fall Special Olympics
St. Augustine High School

English tutor
Flagler College
Fall/Spring 2003

Fantasy football writer
www.fantasysportsjunkies.com
June 2005 - January 2006

RESUME

SUMMARY OF QUALIFICATIONS

Dedicated and self-motivated individual offering a
services, and inventory management, with extensive
excellent communication, organization and multi-ta
contributing member of the team. Consistently aw
rd of achievement in meeting and exceeding custom
cient in Windows 98/XP, Microsoft Office Suite (W
et. Applied experience in database management a

MENT HISTORY

c Assistant
any, City, State
, marketing and administrative operations f
generating $300K in annual revenue and ser
al office administration and e-commerce [su
of marketing and customer service program
g and receiving of all inventory. Designed
dened inventory control and replaced a p
contact system that substantially improve
mmunications programs.

Sample Federal Cover Letters

Street address
City, State ZIP
Phone number
E-mail

October 21, 2010

Contact name
Address

Dear Sir or Madam:

I have more than three years' experience in a mental health setting, working with youth who had any variety of mental health and/or substance abuse diagnoses. I know the field well, and I know the people who work in the field. After reading the job posting for this position, I immediately knew I was the perfect candidate for the job.

I have the ability to work well with all sorts of people and to bring a grit and determination to the position that very few others would. My experience working in the field gives an entirely different view than for most. I more than exceed your requirement of a diploma, in that I have a bachelor's degree in justice studies from State University. I have a perfectly clean driving and criminal record as well. I am the candidate that you are after.

Please feel free to call me at any time on my cell phone at (123) 456-7890 or e-mail me at langon@email.com to arrange an interview. Thank you for your consideration in this matter.

Sincerely,
Logan R. Andress

1234 Boulevard Street
City, State ZIP
Phone number
E-mail

October 21, 2010

Contact name
Address

Dear Sir or Madam:

I believe that I am uniquely qualified for the open program manager position. Not only do I bring nearly six years of experience in the field to you, but I also bring it to you from various aspects within the field. I have worked direct care, I have written individual plans, and I have supervised staff, all while working within the field itself.

Further, not only do I bring that to the table, but I also bring a dedication that I vow will be unmatched. If there is one thing that I have learned in this job, it is that intelligence and creativity are great, but they are useless without proper instincts and a true care for the people that we work with. It is that view that will make me standout to you among the applicants you will review.

I look forward to hearing from you to arrange an interview. Please feel free to contact me at any time on my cell phone at (123) 456-7890 to arrange an interview. Enclosed, please find a copy of my résumé for your review. Thank you in advance for your consideration in this matter.

Sincerely,
Sara M. Hartmann, B.S.

Joe Ferrier

123 Boulevard Street
City, State ZIP
(123) 456-7890

February 24, 2009

Hiring Manager
Department of Defense

Dear Hiring Manager:

Being fluent in French, German, Spanish, and Russian, I believe you will find my language skills extremely useful as your international editorial assistant that was advertised on the USAJOBS website.

I am a recent graduate from a master's program in international relations at Columbia. As a student of political and social sciences, I research, write, and edit a large number of papers on a variety of topics. I have more than two years of administrative background and two years of experience working for my community's newspaper. In high school, I was actively involved in my school's yearbook and newspaper and served as editor-in-chief of the school's literary magazine. I believe my varied background and interests will prove an asset to your publishing firm.

I am a creative, motivated candidate, who is organized and able to multitask. I love a challenge and am used to working under deadlines. Through my extensive work on research papers for my degrees and various customer service-oriented jobs, I have developed exceptional written and oral communications skills. As an avid reader, I would bring a personal passion to the job.

Thank you for your time and consideration. I will be in New York in two weeks visiting family and hope to speak with you at that time. I will call Monday to schedule an appointment per your availability.

Respectfully,

Joe Ferrier

Sarah Jones
123 Boulevard Street
City, State ZIP
123-456-7890

March 20, 2009

Frank White
U.S. Department of Housing and Urban Development
123 Boulevard Street
City, State ZIP

Dear Frank White

Per your conversation with our mutual friend, Beth Walters, I am forwarding my résumé for your evaluation. After my graduation in May with my M.B.A, I wish to participate in your commercial credit training program and continue as a credit officer for your institution, putting to work my education and your training immediately.

My résumé highlights my academic achievements, including my B.A. in finance and experience as the student body treasurer, as well as my work for Wachovia, where I worked for Ms. Walters for several years as a teller/head teller while working my way through my undergraduate.

I would like to demonstrate my ability to succeed with your bank. I know Ms. Walters has given me her strongest recommendation. She has thought highly of me since I started working for her as a part-time teller out of high school. However, I wish to make such an impression on you and believe that can only be done with a personal interview. Therefore, I will contact your secretary next week to schedule an appointment with you so we can further discuss how I can make a positive contribution to your company once my training with you is complete.

Best Regards,

Sarah Jones

APPENDIX C

Federal Agencies, Departments, Divisions, and Organizations

- Administration for Children and Families (ACF)
- Administration for Native Americans
- Administration on Aging
- Administration on Developmental Disabilities
- Administrative Committee of the Federal Register
- Administrative Office of the U.S. Courts
- Advisory Office on Historical Preservation

- African Development Foundation
- Agency for Healthcare Research and Quality
- Agency for International Development
- Agency for Toxic Substances and Disease Registry
- Agricultural Marketing Service
- Agricultural Research Service
- Agriculture Department (USDA)
- Air Force

- Alcohol, Tobacco, Firearms, and Explosives Bureau
- Alcohol and Tobacco Tax and Trade Bureau
- American Battle Monuments Commission
- AMTRAK (National Railroad Passenger Corporation)
- Animal and Plant Health Inspection Service
- Architect of the Capitol
- Architectural and Transportation Barriers Compliance Board
- National Archives and Records Administration
- Arctic Research Commission
- Armed Forces Retirement Home
- Arms Control and International Security
- Army
- Army Corps of Engineers
- Atlantic Fleet Forces Command
- Bonneville Power Administration
- Botanic Garden
- Broadcasting Board of Governors
- Bureau of Citizenship and Immigration Services
- Bureau of Economic Analysis
- Bureau of Engraving and Printing
- Bureau of Indian Affairs
- Bureau of Industry and Security
- Bureau of International Labor Affairs
- Bureau of Justice Statistics
- Bureau of Labor Statistics
- Bureau of Land Management
- Bureau of Prisons
- Bureau of Public Debt
- Bureau of Reclamation
- Bureau of Census
- Bureau of Transportation Statistics
- Capitol Visitors Center
- Census Bureau
- Center for Nutrition Policy and Promotion
- Centers for Disease Control and Prevention
- Centers for Medicare & Medicaid Services
- Central Command
- Central Intelligence Agency

- Chemical Safety and Hazard Investigation Board
- Chief Acquisition Officers Council
- Chief Financial Officers Council
- Chief Human Capital Officers Council
- Chief Information Officers Council
- Citizen's Stamp Advisory Committee
- Citizenship and Immigration Services Bureau
- Civilian Radioactive Waste Management
- Coast Guard
- Commerce Department
- Commission of Fine Arts
- Commission on Civil Rights
- Commission on International Religious Freedom
- Commission on Security and Cooperation in Europe
- Committee for Purchase from People Who Are Blind or Severally Disabled
- Committee for the Implementation of Textile Agreements
- Committee on Foreign Investments in the United States
- Commodity Futures Trading Commission
- Community Oriented Policing Services
- Community Planning and Development
- Comptroller of the Currency Office
- Computer Emergency Readiness Team
- Congress
- Congressional Budget Office
- Congressional Research Service
- Constitution Center
- Consumer Product Safety Commission
- Coordinating Council on Juvenile Justice and Delinquency Prevention
- Copyright Office
- Corporation for National and Community Service
- Corps of Engineers
- Council of Economic Advisers
- Council on Environmental Quality
- County and City Governments

- Court of Appeals for the Armed Forces
- Court of Appeals for the Federal Circuit
- Court of Appeals for Veterans Claims
- Court of Federal Claims
- Court of International Trade
- Court Services and Offender Supervision Agency for the District of Columbia
- Customs and Border Protection
- National Institute of Food and Agriculture
- Defense Acquisition University
- Defense Advanced Research Projects Agency (DARPA)
- Defense Commissary Agency
- Defense Contract Audit Agency (DCAA)
- Defense Contract Management Agency
- Defense Department (DOD)
- Defense Field Activities
- Defense Finance and Accounting Service (DFAS)
- Defense Information Systems Agency (DISA)
- Defense Intelligence Agency (DIA)

- Defense Legal Services Agency
- Defense Logistics Agency (DLA)
- Defense Nuclear Facilities Safety Board
- Defense Security Cooperation Agency (DSCA)
- Defense Security Service (DSS)
- Defense Technical Information Center
- Defense Threat Reduction Agency (DTRA)
- Denali Commission
- Department of Agriculture (USDA)
- Department of Commerce (DOC)
- Department of Defense (DOD)
- Department of Defense Inspector General
- Department of Education (ED)
- Department of Energy (DOE)
- Department of Health and Human Services (HHS)
- Department of Homeland Security (DHS)
- Department of Housing and Urban Development (HUD)
- Department of Justice (DOJ)

- Department of Labor (DOL)
- Department of State (DOS)
- Department of the Interior (DOI)
- Department of the Treasury
- Department of Transportation (DOT)
- Department of Veterans Affairs (VA)
- Director of National Intelligence
- Domestic Policy Council
- Drug Enforcement Administration (DEA)
- Economic, Business and Agricultural Affairs (State Department)
- Economic Adjustment Office
- Economic Analysis, Bureau of
- Economic Development Administration
- Economic Research Service
- Economics & Statistics Administration
- Education Department (ED)
- Election Assistance Commission
- Elementary and Secondary Education
- Employee Benefits Security Administration (formerly Pension and Welfare Benefits Administration)
- Employment and Training Administration (Labor Department)
- Endangered Species Committee
- Energy Department (DOE)
- Energy Efficiency and Renewable Energy
- Energy Information Administration
- English Language Acquisition Office
- Engraving and Printing, Bureau of
- Environmental Management (Energy Department)
- Environmental Protection Agency (EPA)
- Equal Employment Opportunity Commission (EEOC)
- European Command
- Executive Office for Immigration Review
- Export Administration (now the Bureau of Industry and Security)

- Export-Import Bank of the United States
- Fair Housing and Equal Opportunity
- Farm Credit Administration
- Farm Service Agency
- Federal Accounting Standards Advisory Board
- Federal Aviation Administration (FAA)
- Federal Bureau of Investigation (FBI)
- Federal Bureau of Prisons
- Federal Citizen Information Center (FCIC)
- Federal Communications Commission (FCC)
- Federal Consulting Group
- Federal Deposit Insurance Corporation (FDIC)
- Federal Election Commission
- Federal Emergency Management Agency (FEMA)
- Federal Energy Regulatory Commission
- Federal Executive Boards
- Federal Financial Institutions Examination Council
- Federal Financing Bank
- Federal Geographic Data Committee
- Federal Highway Administration
- Federal Housing Enterprise Oversight
- Federal Housing Finance Board
- Federal Interagency Committee for the Management of Noxious and Exotic Weeds
- Federal Interagency Committee on Education
- Federal Interagency Council on Statistical Policy
- Federal Judicial Center
- Federal Laboratory Consortium for Technology Transfer
- Federal Labor Relations Authority
- Federal Law Enforcement Training Center
- Federal Library and Information Center Committee
- Federal Maritime Commission
- Federal Mediation and Conciliation Service
- Federal Mine Safety and Health Review Commission
- Federal Motor Carrier Safety Administration

- Federal Railroad Administration
- Federal Reserve System
- Federal Retirement Thrift Investment Board
- Federal Student Aid
- Federal Trade Commission (FTC)
- Federal Transit Administration
- Federated States of Micronesia Home Page
- Financial Crisis Inquiry Commission
- Financial Management Service (Treasury Department)
- Fiscal Responsibility and Reform, National Commission
- Fish and Wildlife Service
- Food, Nutrition and Consumer Services
- Food and Drug Administration (FDA)
- Food and Nutrition Service
- Food Safety and Inspection Service
- Foreign Agricultural Service
- Foreign Claims Settlement Commission
- Forest Service
- Fossil Energy

- Fulbright Foreign Scholarship Board
- General Services Administration (GSA)
- Geological Survey (USGS)
- Global Affairs (State Department)
- Government Accountability Office (GAO)
- Government National Mortgage Association
- Government Printing Office (GPO)
- Grain Inspection, Packers, and Stockyards Administration
- Health and Human Services Department (HHS)
- Health Resources and Services Administration
- Helsinki Commission (Commission on Security and Cooperation in Europe)
- Holocaust Memorial Museum
- Homeland Security Department (DHS)
- House Leadership Offices
- House Office of Inspector General
- House Office of the Clerk
- House of Representatives

- House of Representatives Committees
- House Organizations, Commissions, and Task Forces
- House Representatives on the Web
- Housing and Urban Development Department (HUD)
- Housing Office (HUD)
- Immigration and Customs Enforcement
- Immigration and Naturalization Service (Bureau of Citizenship and Immigration Services)
- Indian Affairs, Bureau of
- Indian Health Service
- Industrial College of the Armed Forces
- Industry and Security, Bureau of (formerly the Bureau of Export Administration)
- Information Resource Management College
- Innovation and Improvement Office
- Institute of Education Sciences
- Institute of Museum and Library Services
- Institute of Peace

- Interagency Alternative Dispute Resolution Working Group
- Interagency Council on Homelessness
- Inter-American Foundation
- Interior Department
- Internal Revenue Service (IRS)
- International Broadcasting Bureau (IBB)
- International Labor Affairs, Bureau of
- International Trade Administration (ITA)
- International Trade Commission
- Japan-United States Friendship Commission
- John F. Kennedy Center for the Performing Arts
- Joint Board for the Enrollment of Actuaries
- Joint Chiefs of Staff
- Joint Congressional Committee on Inaugural Ceremonies
- Joint Fire Science Program
- Joint Forces Command
- Joint Forces Staff College
- Joint Military Intelligence College

- Judicial Circuit Courts of Appeal, by Geographic Location and Circuit
- Judicial Panel on Multidistrict Litigation
- Justice Department
- Justice Programs Office (Juvenile Justice, Victims of Crime, Violence Against Women and more)
- Justice Statistics, Bureau of
- Labor Department (DOL)
- Labor Statistics, Bureau of
- Land Management, Bureau of
- Lead Hazard Control (Housing and Urban Development Department)
- Legal Services Corporation
- Library of Congress
- Local Governments
- Bureau of Ocean Energy Management, Regulation, and Enforcement (formerly Minerals Management Service)
- Marine Corps
- Marine Mammal Commission
- Maritime Administration
- Marketing and Regulatory Programs (Agriculture Department)
- Marshals Service
- Medicare Payment Advisory Commission
- Merit Systems Protection Board
- Migratory Bird Conservation Commission
- Military Postal Service Agency
- Millennium Challenge Corporation
- Mine Safety and Health Administration
- Minority Business Development Agency
- Mint (Treasury Department)
- Missile Defense Agency (MDA)
- Multifamily Housing Office
- National Aeronautics and Space Administration (NASA)
- National Agricultural Statistics Service
- National AIDS Policy Office
- National Archives and Records Administration (NARA)
- National Bipartisan Commission on the Future of Medicare
- National Capital Planning Commission

- National Cemetery Administration (Veterans Affairs Department)
- National Commission on Fiscal Responsibility and Reform
- National Constitution Center
- National Council on Disability
- National Counterintelligence Executive, Office of
- National Credit Union Administration
- National Defense University
- National Drug Intelligence Center
- National Economic Council
- National Endowment for the Arts
- National Endowment for the Humanities
- National Gallery of Art
- National Geospatial-Intelligence Agency
- National Guard
- National Highway Traffic Safety Administration
- National Indian Gaming Commission
- National Institute for Literacy
- National Institute of Justice
- National Institute of Standards and Technology (NIST)
- National Institutes of Health (NIH)
- National Interagency Fire Center
- National Laboratories (Energy Department)
- National Labor Relations Board
- National Marine Fisheries Service
- National Mediation Board
- National Nuclear Security Administration
- National Oceanic and Atmospheric Administration (NOAA)
- National Ocean Service
- National Park Foundation
- National Park Service
- National Railroad Passenger Corporation (AMTRAK)
- National Reconnaissance Office
- National Science Foundation
- National Security Agency (NSA)
- National Security Council

- National Technical Information Service
- National Telecommunications and Information Administration
- National Transportation Safety Board
- National War College
- National Weather Service
- Natural Resources Conservation Service
- Navy
- Nuclear Energy, Science and Technology
- Nuclear Regulatory Commission
- Nuclear Waste Technical Review Board
- Oak Ridge National Laboratory
- Occupational Safety & Health Administration (OSHA)
- Occupational Safety and Health Review Commission
- Office of Compliance
- Office of Federal Housing Enterprise Oversight
- Office of Government Ethics
- Office of Management and Budget (OMB)

- Office of National Drug Control Policy (ONDCP)
- Office of Personnel Management
- Office of Refugee Resettlement
- Office of Science and Technology Policy
- Office of Scientific and Technical Information
- Office of Special Counsel
- Office of Thrift Supervision
- Open World Leadership Center
- Overseas Private Investment Corporation
- Pacific Command
- Pardon Attorney Office
- Parole Commission (Justice Department)
- Patent and Trademark Office
- Peace Corps
- Pension and Welfare Benefits Administration (now the Employee Benefits Security Administration)
- Pension Benefit Guaranty Corporation
- Pentagon Force Protection Agency
- Pipeline and Hazardous Materials Safety Administration

- Policy Development and Research (Housing and Urban Development Department)
- Political Affairs (State Department)
- Postal Regulatory Commission
- Postal Service (USPS)
- Postsecondary Education
- Power Administrations
- Presidio Trust
- Prisoner of War/Missing Personnel Office
- Public and Indian Housing
- Public Debt, Bureau of
- Public Diplomacy and Public Affairs (State Department)
- Radio and TV Marti (Español)
- Radio Free Asia (RFA)
- Radio Free Europe/Radio Liberty (RFE/RL)
- Railroad Retirement Board
- Reclamation, Bureau of
- Refugee Resettlement
- Regulatory Information Service Center
- Rehabilitation Services Administration (Education Department)
- Research, Education, and Economics (Agriculture Department)
- Research and Innovative Technology Administration (Transportation Department)
- Risk Management Agency (Agriculture Department)
- Rural Business and Cooperative Programs
- Rural Development
- Rural Housing Service
- Rural Utilities Service
- Saint Lawrence Seaway Development Corporation
- Science Office (Energy Department)
- Secret Service
- Securities and Exchange Commission (SEC)
- Selective Service System
- Senate
- Senate Committees
- Senate Leadership
- Senators on the Web
- Small Business Administration (SBA)
- Smithsonian Institution
- Social Security Administration (SSA)

- Social Security Advisory Board
- Southeastern Power Administration
- Southern Command
- Southwestern Power Administration
- Special Education and Rehabilitative Services
- Special Forces Operations Command
- State Agencies by Topic
- State Department
- State Home Pages
- State Justice Institute
- Stennis Center for Public Service
- Strategic Command
- Substance Abuse and Mental Health Services Administration
- Supreme Court of the United States
- Surface Mining, Reclamation and Enforcement
- Surface Transportation Board
- Susquehanna River Basin Commission
- Tax Court
- Taxpayer Advocacy Panel
- Tennessee Valley Authority
- Territories of the United States

- Texas Home Page
- Texas State, County and City Websites
- Transportation Command
- Transportation Department (DOT)
- Transportation Security Administration
- Transportation Statistics, Bureau of
- Treasury Department
- TRICARE Management
- Trustee Program (Justice Department)
- U.S. Border Patrol (now Customs and Border Protection)
- U.S. Capitol Visitor Center
- U.S. Citizenship and Immigration Services
- U.S. Customs and Border Protection
- U.S. Immigration and Customs Enforcement
- U.S. International Trade Commission
- U.S. Military Academy, West Point
- U.S. Mint

- U.S. Mission to the United Nations
- U.S. National Central Bureau — Interpol (Justice Department)
- U.S. Postal Service (USPS)
- U.S. Sentencing Commission
- U.S. Trade and Development Agency
- U.S. Trade Representative
- U.S. Virgin Islands
- Unified Combatant Commands (Defense Department)
- Uniformed Services University of the Health Sciences
- Veterans Affairs Department (VA)
- Veterans Benefits Administration
- Veterans Employment and Training Service
- Veterans Health Administration
- Vietnam Educational Foundation
- Voice of America (VOA)
- Veterans Day National Committee
- Washington Headquarters Services
- Weather Service, National
- Western Area Power Administration
- West Point (Army)
- White House
- White House Commission on the National Moment of Remembrance
- White House Office of Administration
- Women's Bureau (Labor Department)
- Woodrow Wilson International Center for Scholars

APPENDIX D

GS Codes

SALARY TABLE 2010-GS

INCORPORATING THE 1.50% GENERAL SCHEDULE INCREASE

EFFECTIVE JANUARY 2010

Annual Rates by Grade and Step

Grade	Step 1	Step 2	Step 3	Step 4	Step 5	Step 6	Step 7	Step 8	Step 9	Step 10	Within Grade Amounts
1	17803	18398	18990	19579	20171	20519	21104	21694	21717	22269	VARIES
2	20017	20493	21155	21717	21961	22607	23253	23899	24545	25191	VARIES
3	21840	22568	23296	24024	24752	25480	26208	26936	27664	28392	728
4	24518	25335	26152	26969	27786	28603	29420	30237	31054	31871	817
5	27431	28345	29259	30173	31087	32001	32915	33829	34743	35657	914
6	30577	31596	32615	33634	34653	35672	36691	37710	38729	39748	1019
7	33979	35112	36245	37378	38511	39644	40777	41910	43043	44176	1133
8	37631	38885	40139	41393	42647	43901	45155	46409	47663	48917	1254
9	41563	42948	44333	45718	47103	48488	49873	51258	52643	54028	1385
10	45771	47297	48823	50349	51875	53401	54927	56453	57979	59505	1526
11	50287	51963	53639	55315	56991	58667	60343	62019	63695	65371	1676
12	60274	62283	64292	66301	68310	70319	72328	74337	76346	78355	2009
13	71674	74063	76452	78841	81230	83619	86008	88397	90786	93175	2389
14	84697	87520	90343	93166	95989	98812	101635	104458	107281	110104	2823
15	99628	102949	106270	109591	112912	116233	119554	122875	126196	129517	3321

SALARY TABLE 2010-GS

INCORPORATING THE 1.50% GENERAL SCHEDULE INCREASE
EFFECTIVE JANUARY 2010
Hourly/Overtime Rates by Grade and Step

Grade	B/O	Step 1	Step 2	Step 3	Step 4	Step 5	Step 6	Step 7	Step 8	Step 9	Step 10
1	B	8.53	8.82	9.10	9.38	9.67	9.83	10.11	10.39	10.41	10.67
	O	12.80	13.23	13.65	14.07	14.51	14.75	15.17	15.59	15.62	16.01
2	B	9.59	9.82	10.14	10.41	10.52	10.83	11.14	11.45	11.76	12.07
	O	14.39	14.73	15.21	15.62	15.78	16.25	16.71	17.18	17.64	18.11
3	B	10.46	10.81	11.16	11.51	11.86	12.21	12.56	12.91	13.26	13.60
	O	15.69	16.22	16.74	17.27	17.79	18.32	18.84	19.37	19.89	20.40
4	B	11.75	12.14	12.53	12.92	13.31	13.71	14.10	14.49	14.88	15.27
	O	17.63	18.21	18.80	19.38	19.97	20.57	21.15	21.74	22.32	22.91
5	B	13.14	13.58	14.02	14.46	14.90	15.33	15.77	16.21	16.65	17.09
	O	19.71	20.37	21.03	21.69	22.35	23.00	23.66	24.32	24.98	25.64
6	B	14.65	15.14	15.63	16.12	16.60	17.09	17.58	18.07	18.56	19.05
	O	21.98	22.71	23.45	24.18	24.90	25.64	26.37	27.11	27.84	28.58
7	B	16.28	16.82	17.37	17.91	18.45	19.00	19.54	20.08	20.62	21.17
	O	24.42	25.23	26.06	26.87	27.68	28.50	29.31	30.12	30.93	31.76
8	B	18.03	18.63	19.23	19.83	20.43	21.04	21.64	22.24	22.84	23.44
	O	27.05	27.95	28.85	29.75	30.65	31.56	32.46	32.90	32.90	32.90
9	B	19.92	20.58	21.24	21.91	22.57	23.23	23.90	24.56	25.22	25.89
	O	29.88	30.87	31.86	32.87	32.90	32.90	32.90	32.90	32.90	32.90
10	B	21.93	22.66	23.39	24.13	24.86	25.59	26.32	27.05	27.78	28.51
	O	32.90	32.90	32.90	32.90	32.90	32.90	32.90	32.90	32.90	32.90
11	B	24.10	24.90	25.70	26.50	27.31	28.11	28.91	29.72	30.52	31.32
	O	32.90	32.90	32.90	32.90	32.90	32.90	32.90	32.90	32.90	32.90
12	B	28.88	29.84	30.81	31.77	32.73	33.69	34.66	35.62	36.58	37.54
	O	32.90	32.90	32.90	32.90	32.90	33.69	34.66	35.62	36.58	37.54
13	B	34.34	35.49	36.63	37.78	38.92	40.07	41.21	42.36	43.50	44.65
	O	34.34	35.49	36.63	37.78	38.92	40.07	41.21	42.36	43.50	44.65
14	B	40.58	41.94	43.29	44.64	45.99	47.35	48.70	50.05	51.40	52.76
	O	40.58	41.94	43.29	44.64	45.99	47.35	48.70	50.05	51.40	52.76
15	B	47.74	49.33	50.92	52.51	54.10	55.69	57.29	58.88	60.47	62.06
	O	47.74	49.33	50.92	52.51	54.10	55.69	57.29	58.88	60.47	62.06

Federal Job Titles by College Major

Below is a sampling of titles that relate to various college majors. Many of these positions allow for the substitution of experience for a degree. Most of these titles require either a bachelor's degree or five years of closely related experience. A degree in the subject listed does not necessarily meet basic requirements of the position. Some require specific coursework in other subjects and some, such as project manager, require experience.

Titles marked (*) can be entered with no education or experience, but coursework leading to an associate, vocational, or bachelor's degree can qualify workers for a higher level of responsibility and pay.

Finally, there are many other titles related to these subjects, and official titles change with changing regulations. Use this list as a guide, but search for positions by keyword and occupational group, as well.

Agriculture and agronomy

- Agricultural commodity grader
- Agricultural engineer
- Agricultural management specialist
- Agricultural program specialist
- Agronomist
- Foreign agriculture affairs specialist
- Irrigation operation occupation*
- Social conservation technician*
- Soil conservationist
- Soil scientist

Architecture and construction science

- Architect
- Construction analyst
- Construction control inspector
- Landscape architect
- Naval architect

Art

- Arts specialist

- Audio-visual production specialist
- Design patents examiner
- Exhibits specialist or technician
- General arts and information specialist
- Illustrator
- Museum specialist or technician
- Photographer
- Recreation and creative arts therapist
- Visual information specialist

Astronomy

- Astronomer and space scientist
- Geodesist
- Physical scientist

Biology

- Animal health technician*
- Animal scientist
- Biological science technician*
- Biological scientist, general
- Consumer safety specialist

- Fish and wildlife refuge management
- Fishery biologist
- Food inspector
- General fish and wildlife administrator
- Government Accountability Office (GAO) analyst
- Microbiologist
- Range conservationist
- Range technician*
- Veterinarian or veterinary health scientist
- Wildlife biologist
- Zoologist

Botany

- Agronomist
- Botanist
- Forestry technician*
- Geneticist
- Horticulturist
- Plant pathologist
- Plant physiologist
- Plant protection and quarantine specialist
- Plant protection technician*

Business

- Business and industry specialist
- Contract specialist or procurement analyst
- Government Accountability Office (GAO) analyst
- Miscellaneous administrative and programs specialist, including acquisition manager
- Program analyst

Accounting and finance

- Accountant
- Accounting technician*
- Assessor
- Auditor
- Budget analyst
- Financial administrator
- Financial analyst
- Financial institution examiner
- Financial manager
- Government Accountability Office (GAO) evaluator
- Intelligence specialist
- Internal revenue agent or officer

- Securities compliance examiner
- Tax specialist
- Trade specialist

Facilities management and realty

- Distribution facility and storage manager
- Equipment specialist
- Facility manager
- Housing manager
- Industrial property manager
- Realtor

Human resources and employee relations

- Apprenticeship and training representative
- Contractor industrial relations specialist
- Employee development specialist
- Employee relations specialist
- Equal employment opportunity specialist
- Hearing and appeals specialist
- Labor management relations specialist or examiner

- Mediator
- Wage and hour compliance specialist

Industrial management

- Industrial hygienist
- Production control specialist
- Quality assurance specialist

Management

- Administrative officer
- Commissary store manager
- Logistics management specialist
- Management analyst
- Printing manager
- Program manager
- Project manager
- Supply specialist
- Support services administrator

Management information systems

- Financial manager
- Information technology specialist or manager
- Operations research analyst

Marketing

- Agricultural marketing specialist

- Bond sales promotion representative
- Property disposal specialist
- Trade specialist

Chemistry

- Chemical engineer
- Chemist
- Consumer safety officer
- Environmental engineer
- Food inspector
- Food technologist
- Health physicist
- Hospital housekeeping management
- Intelligence specialist
- Physical scientist
- Toxicologist

Communications and journalism

- Agricultural market reporter
- Broadcaster
- Communications specialist
- Language specialist
- Printing manager
- Public affairs specialist
- Technical writer/editor
- Telecommunications managers
- Writer/editor

Computer science

- Computer specialist
- Information technology project manager
- Information technology (covers many specialties)

Counseling and social work

- Educational and vocational training specialist
- Educational services specialist
- Equal opportunity compliance specialist
- Food assistance program specialists and other social program specialists
- Human resources specialist
- Psychologist
- Social service aids and assistant*
- Social insurance administrator
- Social worker
- Vocational rehabilitation specialist

Criminal justice

- Border patrol agent
- Correctional officer
- Criminal investigator

- Document analyst
- Internal revenue officer
- Police officer
- U.S. marshal

Education and library science

Education

- Education and training specialist or technician
- Educational program specialist
- Employee development specialist
- Instructional systems specialist
- Public health educator
- Teacher (U.S. Department of Defense)
- Training instructor
- Vocational rehabilitation specialist

Library science

- Archivist
- Librarian
- Supply cataloger

Physical education

- Outdoor recreation planner
- Recreation specialist
- Sports specialist

Electronics

- Electronics technician*
- Telecommunications manager

English and literature

- Communications analyst
- Miscellaneous administrators and programs specialist
- Printing manager
- Public affairs specialist
- Technical writer/editor
- Writer/editor

Engineering

- Engineering specialties
- Operations research analyst
- Physical scientist
- Quality assurance occupations

Environmental studies

- Ecologist
- Environmental engineer
- Environmental protection assistant*
- Environmental protection specialist

- Fish and wildlife refuge management
- General fish and wildlife administrator
- Government Accountability Office (GAO) analyst
- Programs specialist (Environmental and natural resources)
- Rangeland manager

Foreign language

- Border patrol agent
- Customs inspector
- Foreign affairs specialist
- Intelligence specialist
- Language specialist

Forestry

- Forest products technology specialist
- Forestry specialist
- Forestry technician*
- Soil conservationist

Geology

- Geodesist
- Geologist
- Hydrologist

- Oceanographer
- Physical scientist

Health and medicine

- Consumer safety specialist
- Consumer safety inspector*
- Public health programs specialist

Health science
- Industrial hygienist
- Public health educator
- Safety and occupational health manager
- Social insurance administrator

Hospital administration
- Administrative officer
- Health system administrator
- Health system specialist
- Hospital housekeeping manager

Medical
- Dental hygienist*
- Dental hygienist, community health
- Diagnostic radiological technician*
- Medical officer ("physician"

or specialty name often used)
- Medical technician*
- Nurse
- Pharmacist
- Physical therapist
- Physician assistant

Nutrition
- Consumer safety officer
- Dietitians and nutritionists
- Food assistance program specialist
- Food technology occupations

History
- Archivist
- Historian
- Government Accountability Office (GAO) analyst
- Intelligence specialist
- Museum curator
- Museum specialist
- Miscellaneous administrator and programs specialist

Law
- Administrative law judge
- Attorney

- Hearing and appeals specialist
- Highway safety specialist
- Import specialist
- Paralegal
- Tax law specialist

Mathematics
- Actuary
- Cartographer
- Mathematician
- Operations research analyst
- Statistician
- Traffic manager

Park and recreation management
- Forester
- Outdoor recreation planner
- Park ranger
- Recreation and creative arts therapist
- Recreation specialist

Physics
- Astronomer and space scientist
- Geodesist

- Geophysicist
- Health physicist
- Hydrologist
- Patent examiner
- Photographic technology specialist
- Physical scientist
- Physicist

Social science

- Program specialist
- Social scientist

Archaeology and anthropology
- Anthropologist
- Archaeologist
- Museum curator
- Museum specialist

Economics
- Economist
- Financial analyst
- Industrial analyst
- Manpower development specialist
- Trade specialist

Geography
- Cartographer

- Cartographic technician*
- Community planner
- Geodetic technician
- Geographer
- Intelligence specialist
- Navigational information specialist
- Surveying technician*
- Other titles plus Geographic Information Systems (GIS)

International relations
- Foreign affairs specialist
- Intelligence specialist
- International relations specialist
- International trade specialist
- Language specialist

Political science, government, or public administration
- Foreign affairs specialist
- Government Accountability Office (GAO) analyst
- Miscellaneous administrators and programs specialist
- Program analyst
- Program manager
- Public affairs specialist
- Public utilities manager

Psychology

- Educational services specialist
- Employee development specialist
- Human resources specialist
- Psychologist
- Recreational and creative arts therapist

Sociology

- Social service aids and assistant*
- Social service administration specialist
- Sociologist

Common titles across all majors

- Intelligence specialist
- Program analyst
- Program manager
- Program specialist
- Writer/editor

Learn More Resources

For more information about the application process, contact the U.S. Office of Personnel Management. This office has created several publications for job seekers. It also publishes employment regulations, job descriptions, qualifications manuals, and statistics about federal employment. Contact:

U. S. Office of Personnel Management
1900 E St. NW
Washington, DC 20415-0001
(202) 606-1800
TTY: (202) 606-2532
www.opm.gov
(Employment information site: **www.opm.usajobs.gov/**)

The U.S. Office of Personnel Management also maintains websites for specific types of job seekers:

- **www.studentjobs.gov** provides information about jobs for students.

- **www.opm.gov/disability** provides information tailored to applicants who are disabled.

- **www.opm.gov/veterans** provides information about how military skills relate to civilian jobs in the federal government and about applying for hiring preferences.

- **www.opm.gov/employ/diversity/hispanic** provides information about the bilingual or bicultural employment program.

The Partnership for Public Service is another source of information. This nonprofit organization encourages college graduates to work for the federal government. It publishes advice for students on how to get internships and permanent jobs. Many of its resources are customized for people with specific majors. The partnership also conducts research on federal employment and assists career counselors and federal recruiters. Contact the partnership at:

Partnership for Public Service
1725 Eye St. NW, Suite 900
Washington, DC 20006
(202) 775-9111
www.ourpubicservice.org

For current research on employment practices in the federal government, see the reports and newsletters of the U.S. Merit Systems Protection Board. Contact the board at:

U.S. Merit Systems Protection Board
1615 M St. NW
Washington, DC 20419
Toll-free: (800) 209-8960
www.mspb.gov

Libraries and career centers also provide information on the federal government, including books about how to get government jobs. When choosing books, look for those with recent publication dates because employment regulations change from time to time.

At the library, you also might find two publications from the Bureau of Labor Statistics: the *Occupational Outlook Handbook* and the *Career Guide to Industries.* The Handbook describes the job duties, earnings, employment prospects, and training requirements for hundreds of occupations, most of which are found in the federal government. The *Career Guide to Industries* includes information about employment in the federal government as a whole. It describes federal agencies and the industry's earnings, occupations, and employment prospects. The guide is available online at **www.bls.gov/oco**. Below is contact information for major exempted agencies; they are not required to list all of their openings on the USAJOBS database:

Executive branch
U.S. Agency for International
Development
Recruitment Division
M/HR/POD/SP, 2.08, RRB
Washington, DC 20523
(202) 712-0000
www.usaid.gov

Central Intelligence Agency
Office of Human
Resource Management
Washington, DC 20505
Main number: (703) 482-0623
Student employment programs
and recruitment:
Toll-free: (800) 368-3886
www.cia.gov

Defense Intelligence Agency
Civilian Personnel Division
100 MacDill Blvd.
Washington, DC 20340-5100
Toll-free: (800) 526-4629
www.dia.mil

Federal Reserve System,
Board of Governors
20th St. and Constitution Ave.
NW
Washington, DC 20551
(202) 452-3038
Toll-free: (800) 448-4894
www.federalreserve.gov

Federal Bureau of Investigation
J. Edgar Hoover Bldg.
935 Pennsylvania Ave. NW
Washington, DC 20535
(202) 324-3000
www.fbi.gov

Government Accountability Office
441 G St. NW
Washington, DC 20548
(202) 512-6092
www.gao.gov

National Security Agency
College Relations Branch
Fort Meade, MD 20755
Toll-free: (866) 672-4473
www.nsa.gov

Tennessee Valley Authority
Knoxville Office Complex
400 West Summit Hill Drive
Knoxville, TN 37902
(865) 632-2101
www.tva.gov

U.S. Department of State
Human Resources
2401 E St. NW, Suite 518 H
Washington, DC 20522
(202) 261-8888
www.state.gov

U.S. Nuclear Regulatory
Commission
Division of Human Resources
and Employment
Program Branch
Washington, DC 20555
(301) 415-7400
www.nrc.gov

U.S. Postal Service
Contact local branch
www.usps.com/employment

Judicial branch
U.S. Federal Courts
Administrative Office of the
U.S. Courts
Washington, DC 20544
(202) 502-3800

www.uscourts.gov

Legislative branch
Library of Congress
Employment Office
101 Independence Ave. SE.
Washington, DC 20540
(202) 707-5627
www.loc.gov

U.S. House of Representatives
Chief Administrative Officer
Human Resources Division
B72 Ford House Office Bldg.
Washington, DC 20515

U.S. House of Representatives
(all other offices)
B227 Longworth House Office
Bldg.
Washington, DC 20515
(202) 226-4504
www.house.gov

U.S. Senate
Senate Placement Office
Senate Hart Bldg., Room 142
Washington, DC 20510
(202) 224-9167
www.senate.gov

Local addresses and telephone numbers are listed in the blue pages of the telephone book.

GLOSSARY

Agency employee: When federal agencies announce position openings to indicate that only current employees of that agency can apply.

Vacancy announcement: Another term used for "job description."

Area of consideration: Defines who is eligible to apply for a particular position.

Basic qualification: The minimum qualifications needed to be considered for a position.

Best qualified (BQ): The few people who have been chosen among all the applicants for further consideration.

Closed: Indicates a department or agency is no longer accepting applications for a position.

Career Transition Assistance Program (CTAP): A program, required by law, to help assist federal employees who are displaced through no fault of their own. If they are well qualified for positions and reside in the commuting area where a position in their former agency is located, they might get priority over other candidates.

Excepted service: Civilian jobs in the federal government that are not in the competitive service.

Grade: A number representing the level of work performed in a position in relation to all other levels of work within the occupation.

Interagency Career Transition Assistance Program: A program designed to help federal employees who are displaced through no fault of their own.

Open: Indicates a department of an agency is actively recruiting to fill an open position.

Open continuous: Refers to job descriptions that do not have a specific closing date.

Résumé builder: A computer program that walks applicants through the process of creating a résumé.

Veterans preference: Preference given to veterans to give them an advantage during the federal hiring process.

BIBLIOGRAPHY

Avue Central. **www.avuecentral.com**

Carnegie, Dale. *How to Win Friends and Influence People.* New York: Simon & Schuster, 1936.

"Cover letters: types and samples." Virginia Tech, May 5, 2010. **http://www.career.vt.edu/JobSearchGuide/CoverLetterSamples. html**. Accessed June 10, 2010.

Cox, Bob. E-mail interview by author.

"Executive Order: Employment of Veterans in the Federal Government." The White House, November 9, 2009. **http://www.whitehouse.gov/ the-press-office/executive-order-veterans-employment-initiative**. Accessed August 18, 2010.

"Executive Order – Increasing Federal Employment of Individuals with Disabilities." The White House, July 26, 2010. **http://www.whitehouse.gov/the-press-office/executive-order- increasing-federal-employment-individuals-with-disabilities**. Accessed August 18, 2010.

"Federal Government." Bureau of Labor Statistics. **http://www.bls.gov/oco/cg/cgs041.htm**. Accessed May 5, 2010.

Feds Hire Vets. **www.fedshirevets.gov**

Giddings, Zack. E-mail interview by author.

Harkins, Matt. Phone interview by author.

Hartmann, Sara. Phone interview by author.

Jacovetti, Jennifer. E-mail interview by author.

"Labor Force Statistics from the Current Population Survey." Bureau of Labor Statistics. **http://www.bls.gov/cps/**. Accessed May 5, 2010.

Mathies, Cathy. Phone interview by author.

"Memorandum for Chief Human Capital Officers." United States Office of Personnel Management. **http://www.chcoc.gov/Transmittals/ TransmittalDetails.aspx?TransmittalId=2599**. Accessed September 4, 2010.

Office of Personnel Management. **www.opm.gov**

Parker, Dustin. Phone interview by author.

Parker, Robert. E-mail interview by author.

"Presidential Memorandum — Extension of Benefits to Same-sex Domestic Partners of Federal Employees." June 2, 2010. **http://a. abcnews.go.com/images/Politics/2010benefits_mem_rel.pdf**. Accessed August 18, 2010.

"Presidential Memorandum — Improving the Federal Recruitment and Hiring Process." The White House, May 11, 2010. **http://www. whitehouse.gov/the-press-office/presidential-memorandum- improving-federal-recruitment-and-hiring-process**. Accessed June 29, 2010.

"Presidential Memorandum — Task Force on Space Industry Workforce 1 and Economic Development." The White House May 3, 2010. **http://www.whitehouse.gov/the-press-office/**

presidential-memoranda-task-force-space-industry-workforce-and-economic-development. Accessed August 18, 2010.

"Presidential Memorandum — the Presidential POWER Initiative Protecting Our Workers and Ensuring Reemployment, The White House." July 19, 2010. http://www.whitehouse.gov/the-press-office/presidential-memorandum-presidential-power-initiative-protecting-our-workers-and-en. Accessed August 18, 2010.

Recovery.gov. www.recovery.gov

Shaw, Bransford & Roth, P.C. "Department of Labor Clarifies FMLA Definition of 'Son and Daughter' to Permit Employee to Care for child Regardless of Legal or biological Relationship." *FedManager,* June 29, 2010. http://www.fedmanager.com/article.php?ID=1734. Accessed June 29, 2010.

"Student Educational Employment Program." Office of Personnel Management. http://www.opm.gov/employ/students/intro.asp. Accessed August 31, 2010.

Taylor, Karol and Ruck, Janet. *Guide to America's Federal Jobs.* Indianapolis, Indiana: JIST Publishing, 2009.

Troutman, Kathryn. *Federal Resume Guidebook.* Baltimore, Maryland: The Résumé Place, 2007.

———. *Ten Steps to a Federal Job: How to Land a Job in the Obama Administration.* Baltimore, Maryland: The Résumé Place, 2009.

Waggoner, Erik. Phone interview by author.

Whiteman, Lily. *How to Land a Top-Paying Federal Job.* New York: American Management Association, 2008.

USAJOBS, www.usajobs.opm.gov

AUTHOR
BIOGRAPHY

Melanie Williamson first became interested in the federal employment system while visiting her sister at the federal prison in which she worked. At Bowling Green State University, Williamson studied history and government and worked as a writing consultant at the on-campus writer's lab, giving her opportunities to help other students write their résumés and cover letters. In 2008, she pursued a full-time career in writing, but she still volunteers her time to others who are looking for employment by helping them create their résumés and cover letters.

INDEX